The Effective School Governor

Joan Dean

London and New York

First published 2001 by RoutledgeFalmer
11 New Fetter Lane, London EC4P 4EE

Simultaneously published in the USA and Canada
by RoutledgeFalmer
29 West 35th Street, New York, NY 10001

RoutledgeFalmer is an imprint of the Taylor & Francis Group

© 2001 Joan Dean

Typeset in Goudy by
Florence Production Ltd, Stoodleigh, Devon
Printed and bound in Great Britain by
TJ International Ltd, Padstow, Cornwall

British Library Cataloguing in Publication Data
A catalogue record for this book is available from the British Library

Library of Congress Cataloging in Publication Data
Dean, Joan
  The Effective School Governor / Joan Dean
    p cm.
  Includes bibliographical references and index.
  1. School boards–Great Britain–Handbooks, manuals, etc.
  2. School boards members–Great Britain–Handbooks, manuals, etc.
  3. Educational leadership–Great Britain–Handbooks, manuals, etc.
  4. School management and organization–Great Britain–Handbooks,
  manuals, etc. I. Title.
  LB2831 .D294 2001
  379.1'531'0941–dc21   00–034465

ISBN 0–415–22350–4 (hbk) ✓
ISBN 0–415–22351–2 (pbk)

90 0487297 1

The Effective School Governor

From the best-selling author of key education texts comes Joan Dean's latest management book. Looking at current responsibilities facing school governors, this concise guide offers, sound, realistic advice on how to be effective and efficient. Beginning with an overview of what recent research tells us about the work of governors in schools, the book goes on to discuss practical issues such as:

- developing a statement of vision
- writing a curriculum policy
- appointing new staff
- monitoring the work of the school
- managing finance
- marketing the school
- building relationships with parents
- governor training and evaluation
- managing the premises

The Effective School Governor will be of great interest to governors, head-teachers and LEAs.

Joan Dean has been a headteacher, a primary school adviser and a chief inspector and is currently a governor of her local secondary school. She has published over thirty books for teachers and in 1980 was awarded the OBE for her services to education.

Also available

Improving the Primary School   *Joan Dean*

'If you need one volume on school improvement that'll replace a years' worth of NPQH Compulsory Module notes, buy this one.' – Managing Schools Today

A practical and informative guide on how to improve your primary school, aimed at those in leadership positions.
1998: 184pp
Paperback: 0-415-16895-3   £15.99

Managing Special Needs in the Primary School   *Joan Dean*

'A useful book which provides sound, practical advice to schools about both their obligations to children with SEN as well as helpful ideas about ways of organising and providing efficient support for them.' – Support for Learning

Educational Management
1995: 208pp
Paperback: 0-415-13030-1   £15.99

Organising Learning in the Primary School Classroom, 2nd Edition
Joan Dean

How can primary teachers best use limited time and resources?
How should they respond to the National Curriculum?

'[Joan Dean's] considerable ability to absorb ideas, analyse and organise the information lead to a clear exposition. Add to that her preference for plain language and it is no surprise, though it is a pleasure, that this book is so readable.' – Education Today

1991: 288pp
Paperback: 0-415-06249-7   £13.99

To the Headteacher, Staff and Governors
of St Crispin's School, Wokingham,
who have been the inspiration for this book

Contents

Abbreviations and acronyms

AS	Advanced Subsidiary Level
AST	Advanced Skills Teacher
DES	Department of Education and Science
DfEE	Department for Education and Employment
EFL	English as a Foreign Language
E2L	English as a Second Language
EWO	Educational Welfare Officer
GCSE	General Certificate of Secondary Education
GNVQ	General National Vocational Qualification
GTC	General Teaching Council
HE	Health Education, Home Economics or Higher Education
HMI	Her Majesty's Inspector(s)
ICT	Information and Communication Technology
IEP	Individual Education Plan (for a pupil with special educational needs)
INSET	In-Service Education of Teachers
LEA	Local Education Authority
LMS	Local Management of Schools
MFL	Modern Foreign Language
NAHT	National Association of Headteachers
NASUWT	National Association of Schoolmasters and Union of Women Teachers
NFER	National Foundation for Educational Research
NLS	National Literacy Strategy
NNS	National Numeracy Strategy
NPQH	National Professional Qualification for Headteachers
NQT	Newly Qualified Teacher
NUT	National Union of Teachers
NVQ	National Vocational Qualification
Ofsted	Office for Standards in Education
PE	Physical Education
PGCE	Postgraduate Certificate of Education
PSHE	Personal, Social and Health Education
PTA	Parent–Teacher Association

PTR	Pupil–Teacher Ratio
QCA	Qualifications and Curriculum Authority
QTS	Qualified Teacher Status
RE	Religious Education
RSG	Revenue Support Grant
SACRE	Standing Advisory Committee for Religious Education
SAN	Standard Admission Number
SAT	Standard Assessment Task
SDP	School Development Plan
SEN	Special Educational Needs
SENCO	Special Educational Needs Coordinator
SHA	Secondary Heads Association
SSA	Standard Spending Assessment
STRB	School Teachers' Review Body
SWOT	Strength, Weaknesses, Opportunities and Threats
TES	*Times Educational Supplement*
TSS	Teachers' Superannuation Scheme
UCAS	Universities and Colleges Admissions Service

Chapter 1

Introduction

Jane Dobson was a new governor. She had been elected by the parents at the school where her two children were pupils and was looking forward to her first meeting with mixed feelings. She felt very responsible as a representative of the parents and hoped that she would be able to contribute to the work of the governing body. The chair of the governors, John Robinson, had telephoned to welcome her as soon as he heard of her election and told her that Mary Jamieson, another parent governor, would be acting as her mentor for her first few weeks as a governor. Mary would tell her about the work of the governors and would answer any questions she might have. He also described the committee structure and suggested that she might like to go to any of the committee meetings which interested her so that she would be in a position to decide which ones she would like to join. Most governors were members of two committees and much of the work of the governors was done in committee.

In the days that followed Jane received the governors' file of information. This included the following:

- a copy of the Instrument of Government
- a list of the governors, a thumb-nail sketch of each, their addresses, telephone numbers, email addresses and membership of the various committees
- the terms of reference of the various committees
- a list of the governors' meetings for the next year
- the last annual report from the governors to parents
- the school prospectus
- a plan of the school
- a list of the school staff
- copies of the various school policies
- a short paper on the National Curriculum and another on special needs
- a copy of the Department for Education and Employment (DfEE 1997) publication *School Governors: A Guide to the Law*
- information about courses which would be available for new governors
- copies of the minutes of the last two governors' meetings.

Jane spent quite a bit of time reading all these documents and felt that she was beginning to get a picture of the work of the governing body and the school and at the same time wondered about how much she had taken on.

At the first meeting she attended, the chair of each committee gave a short talk about the work of his or her committee and this helped Jane to decide which committees she would like to join.

Why have governors?

Any organisation which is publicly funded needs to be accountable in some way to the public it serves. Schools are no exception and governing bodies are part of the process of accountability. They have legal status as corporate bodies rather than as individuals. The size and composition of governing bodies is legally determined. Individual governors are appointed by different groups of people but are representatives, not delegates.

Governors are appointed to oversee and support what goes on in schools. The headteacher is responsible for the day-to-day running of the school but is accountable to the governors. Governors appoint the headteacher and staff and determine the aims of the school. They make or approve the policies on which the school is run. They manage the school budget with the headteacher. They bring to the school decision making an independent perspective and experience. They can act as a sounding board for new ideas put forward by the head and staff or suggested by external sources. They support the headteacher and staff in their work and represent the school in the local community.

The history of governing bodies

There have been governors or their equivalent for schools for a long period. In 1833 when education was first supported in part by public funds, the concept of a committee made up of people representing the community served by the school was introduced. In 1870 a national system of public education with locally elected boards was established, the forerunners of local education authorities (LEAs) which had responsibility for building schools and raising local rates for the purpose where church provision was insufficient The schools so established had to have their own boards of managers. In 1902 local education authorities were set up to take over the running of publicly funded schools.

The 1994 Education Act gave the right to free primary and secondary education to all children and gave LEAs the duty and the power to provide education and ancillary services. Instruments and Articles of government for schools were set out in 1945 with help from a model from the Ministry of Education. These gave managers (of primary schools) and governors (of secondary schools) the care of the premises, involvement in the appointment of the headteacher and staff of the school and the general direction of its conduct and curriculum.

In the years following the 1944 Act many primary schools were governed as a group and in some LEAs a subcommittee of the council was responsible for governing all the primary schools in the area. In 1977, the Taylor report A New Partnership for Our Schools (Department of Education and Science and Welsh Office 1977) surveyed the role of governors and managers and recommended that:

One body should have delegated responsibility for running the school, and in forming that body no one interest should be dominant – it should be a partnership of all those with a legitimate concern, local education authority, staff, parents, where appropriate pupils and the community.

(para 6 (iii))

The report saw the governors or managers as having responsibility not only for a certain amount of decision making but also for promoting good relationships within the school and between the school and parents and community. Each school should have its own governing or managing body which 'should stand in the direct line of formal responsibility between the local education authority and the head of the school' (para 3. 15). Governors and managers should normally be appointed for a four year period.

The Taylor Report suggested that people not involved in education had an important contribution to make to how schools were run and they should be responsible for establishing the school's aims, considering how these were translated into practice, keeping progress towards them under review and taking action to facilitate such progress where necessary. Governors were to determine policy, have an equal say with the local authority in the appointment of headteachers, have overall responsibility for staff appointments, make budget decisions and ensure communication with parents.

The 1980 Education Act made the headteacher of a school a member of its governing body unless he or she chose otherwise. The term 'managers' was to be replaced by 'governors' for all schools. The governing body should include at least two governors, who have themselves children at the school, to be elected by the parents. There should also be one or two teacher governors, depending on the size of the school, elected by the teaching staff. It would be possible still for two schools to share a governing body.

The 1986 Education Act laid down that parents were to have equal representation with the LEA (two to five members each, depending on the size of the school). LEA members were to be nominated by the LEA and parent members elected by the parents of children at the school. There were to be between three and six members co-opted from the local community and teachers were to have one or two elected representatives. In church schools there would be foundation governors appointed by the voluntary body whose task was partly to ensure that the school was run according to the trust deed. Governors were to report annually to parents at a special meeting called for the purpose.

In 1988 the Education Reform Act was published. This introduced for the first time a National Curriculum and also made it possible for schools, if governors and parents so decided, to opt out of local authority control and become grant-maintained. This Act gave governors responsibility for the school budget, headteacher and staff appointments, headteacher's and deputy headteacher's pay, overseeing the introduction of the National Curriculum and the operation of the national assessment system.

The option for schools to become grant-maintained has since been withdrawn by the Standards and Framework Act of 1998, which required schools to become community schools, foundation schools or voluntary schools. Schools which had remained with the local authority were most likely to become community schools. Grant-maintained schools were to become foundation schools, going back to being part of the LEA provision but retaining some of the freedom they had formerly. Voluntary schools were those which are aided or controlled by the churches.

The current situation

In September 1999, when schools entered a new legal category under the Standards and Framework Act, each school needed a new Instrument of Government which set out the name of the school and its governing body and its composition. The composition of governing bodies for community schools is shown in Table 1.1. Primary schools with more than a hundred on roll can choose columns c or d. Those with under a hundred children on roll can choose columns e or f.

Primary schools which serve one or more minor authority areas must co-opt one additional governor nominated by one or more of these minor authorities (town, parish or district councils). The governing body of any school with a sponsor may include one or two co-opted governors nominated by the sponsor or sponsors of the school. If the school is in an Education Action Zone, the governing body may include an additional co-opted governor nominated by the forum.

Staff governors who are not teachers may be elected by and from the non-teaching staff at the school. People employed under a contract of employment for services are eligible as well as people in permanent employment. Staff governors must resign if they leave the school.

The composition of governing bodies for foundation schools is shown in Table 1.2.

As with community schools, primary schools with more than a hundred on roll can choose columns c or d. Those with under a hundred children on roll can choose columns e or f.

The composition of governing bodies for voluntary controlled schools is shown in Table 1.3.

Primary schools over a hundred can again choose between columns c and d and those with fewer on roll can choose between columns e and f.

Table 1.1 Composition of governing bodies for community schools

	Secondary schools		Primary schools			
Size of school	600+	fewer than 600	100+		fewer than 100	
	a	b	c	d	e	f
Parent	6	5	5	4	3	3
LEA	5	4	4	3	2	2
Teacher	2	2	2	1	1	1
Other staff	1	1	1	1	1	0
Co-opted	5	4	4	3	2	2
Headteacher	1	1	1	1	1	1

The composition of governing bodies for voluntary aided schools is shown in Table 1.4.

In an aided school the foundation governors are additional to those listed above and must outnumber the other governors by three in the case of a secondary school with six hundred or more on roll or by two in every other case. Primary schools can choose between columns c and d if they are over a hundred and between e and f if they are smaller than this.

Governors serve for four years. In the case of teacher governors, a teacher governor must resign if he or she leaves the school. Parent governors, on the other hand, may continue in office until the end of their four year term even if they no longer have a child at the school.

The headteacher may choose whether or not he or she becomes a governor but is entitled to attend all governing body meetings.

The 1977 Taylor Report suggested that in secondary schools pupils might be members of the governing body. This has not been taken up by government but a number of secondary schools arrange for senior pupils to attend governors' meetings as observers who may report on student views on agreed topics.

The Standards and Framework Act of 1998 lays down the duty of LEAs and governing bodies to have the promotion of high standards as their priority. The LEA has powers to intervene in the running of a school if in the opinion of the LEA pupils' performance is unacceptably low, there is a breakdown in management or discipline or there has not been sufficient improvement in a school designated as having serious weaknesses.

Current employment law makes it possible for employees who are governors of a maintained school or college legally entitled to 'reasonable' (but unpaid) time off work to attend to the duties entailed.

Research into the work of governing bodies

There have been several pieces of research into the work of governing bodies. A House of Commons (1999) Select Committee on Education and Employment report made various suggestions about the work of governing bodies. They commented on the fact that school governors' contribution to the life of British

Table 1.2 Composition of governing bodies for foundation schools

Size of school	Secondary schools		Primary schools			
	600+	fewer than 600	100+		fewer than 100	
	a	b	c	d	e	f
Parent	7	6	5	6	4	4
Foundation	5	4	3	4	2	2
LEA	2	2	2	2	2	2
Teacher	2	2	1	1	1	1
Other staff	1	1	1	1	1	0
Co-opted	3	2	1	1	1	1
Headteacher	1	1	1	1	1	1

Table 1.3 Composition of governing bodies for voluntary controlled schools

| Size of school | Secondary schools | | Primary schools | | | |
| | 600+ | fewer than 600 | 100+ | | fewer than 100 | |
	a	b	c	d	e	f
Parent	6	5	4	5	3	3
Foundation	5	4	3	4	2	2
LEA	4	3	3	3	2	2
Teacher	2	2	1	1	1	1
Other staff	1	1	1	1	1	0
Co-opted	2	2	1	1	1	1
Headteacher	1	1	1	1	1	1

Table 1.4 Composition of governing bodies for voluntary aided schools

| Size of school | Secondary schools | | Primary schools | | | |
| | 600+ | fewer than 600 | 100+ | | fewer than 100 | |
	a	b	c	d	e	f
Parent	3	2	1	2	1	1
LEA	2	1	1	2	1	1
Teacher	2	2	1	1	1	1
Other staff	1	1	1	1	1	0
Headteacher	1	1	1	1	1	1

schools has been too little appreciated and supported the government's emphasis that the governing body's main purpose should be to help raise standards of achievement in schools; they suggested that governors should devote one meeting annually to reviewing standards of achievement in their schools.

Keys and Fernandez (1990) surveyed the views of 2,686 governors in 1,134 primary and secondary schools in England. They found that 44 per cent (35 per cent in primary schools) had a degree or professional institute final qualification. The median time spent by governors on the work of the governing body was about ten hours a term; 22 per cent of governors felt that the most rewarding part of the role was being involved in the life and work of the school. Other rewarding activities were being involved in the decision-making process and appointing staff and other personnel issues. The most time-consuming part of the role was the paperwork.

Over half (54 per cent) of governors thought that the amount of responsibility carried by governors was about right, while 42 per cent thought it too much and 5 per cent too little. Headteachers were also surveyed and between 60 and 70 per cent thought the responsibilities were too high, particularly those for finance, appointments and the National Curriculum. Governors themselves in some cases also thought that these were the areas where the responsibilities were too high.

Earley (1994) followed up the research by Keys and Fernandez (1990) some four years later to see what progress had been made. He sent questionnaires to the headteacher, chair of governors and one other governor in nearly 700 schools, asking some of the same questions as the earlier research and some additional ones.

He found that 55 per cent of headteachers and 70 per cent of chairs thought that their governing bodies had the necessary expertise to carry out the expected role, but inner-city schools were significantly more likely than other schools to lack general management experience, finance, accountancy and budgetary skills.

There was a general feeling that commitment was most important. Heads and chairs communicated with each other about once a week. All three categories of correspondent thought that the most significant contribution of the governing body was providing support for the headteacher and staff. There were hardly any references to policy making. One primary head described the role as follows: 'The governing body provides a lay person's overview that supports the school in a practical way – week by week involvement that puts parents' criticism into perspective and helps the management to stay realistic' (Earley 1994: 30).

Approximately two-thirds of headteachers thought that the responsibilities of governors were too great. This view was shared by about half the chairs and one-third of governors. Generally people felt that they were too wide-ranging. Headteachers in particular referred to the curriculum and decision making/policy making as areas where governors had too much responsibility.

> Over eight out of ten heads, chairs and governors 'agreed' or 'strongly agreed' that their school governors were 'well informed about internal management decisions and events', 'clear about the head's role and responsibilities', and 'very supportive of the work of the school'.
>
> (Earley 1994: 36)

There was also a high level of agreement by all three parties that the governing body was fully involved in discussing policy.

This study echoed the findings of Keys and Fernandez (1990) in concluding that the most rewarding aspects of being a governor were to do with the relationships formed with children and staff and other governors and seeing the school make progress. The study found that the most difficult part of the job was responsibility for personnel, particularly issues such as redundancy, incompetence and determination of salaries.

Earley (1994) asked correspondents about the features of an effective governing body. High on the list for all three groups was the readiness to give time and commitment to supporting the school, staff and pupils, visiting to see the school at work and acting as a critical friend. They also felt that it was important that governors were knowledgeable about educational issues and represented a balance of skills and expertise as well as being representative of the local community. Teamwork was important both within the governing body and with the headteacher and staff of the school. The effective governing body also ran effective meetings that were not too long, were well attended and purposeful.

The study quotes the chair of a primary school as follows:

> Very often schools are like little islands in the middle of their communities. They often don't know what the temperature is outside; how parents see the

school and the difficulties they have in understanding what the children are being taught and why in that way. We get to talk to lots of them outside in other situations.

(Earley 1994: 90)

Deem et al. (1995) studied governors in ten schools in two LEAs. These included a wide variety of governing bodies with some from schools with a high proportion of pupils from ethnic minorities.

They found that the average time spent on school business by individual governors was about two hours a week, rising to five hours in weeks when there were meetings. They noted the issues discussed in meetings and found that the governing bodies they studied rarely included any sustained discussion or decision making about educational issues and learning and teaching. 'The absence of debate on teaching and learning arose both from lay governors' feelings that they lacked the knowledge to intervene in discussion and from determined attempts by heads and teachers to maintain professional boundaries' (Deem et al. 1995: 83). They also found that there were often differences of philosophy between governors and the professionals in the schools they governed and that when governors raised issues of teaching and learning there was a tendency for heads and teachers to become defensive. Children's and young people's perceptions of the educational process were rarely considered by any of the governing bodies they studied.

They asked what governors most enjoyed about their role and found that 'most emphasised partnership with teachers and heads, service to the community, using their skills in a new context, feeling part of the school and gaining more understanding about how education worked' (Deem et al 1995: 42). The things they liked least were the number of papers to be read, the length of meetings and their organisation and the difficulty of understanding educational jargon.

Questions to consider

1   What arrangements have we for welcoming new members of our governing body? What information do we give them? Is there a mentoring system?
2   Are there any areas of skill or knowledge which we should look for in co-opting governors?
3   (Secondary schools) Should we invite representatives of the senior pupils to come to our meetings as observers? If so, should we ask them to find out student views on any particular topics?
4   What are we doing to encourage high standards in our school?
5   Earley (1994) found that few governing bodies discussed policy. Do we discuss and make a sufficient contribution to policy making?
6   Deem et al. (1995) found that few governing bodies discussed education issues and learning and teaching. Do we devote a sufficient amount of time to such issues?
7   What are we doing to discover how pupils feel about what is happening to them in school?

Chapter 2

The knowledge governors need

Governors need knowledge of the following topics.

The rules governing governors' meetings and proceedings

Every governing body must have an Instrument of Government which sets out the rules under which the governing body must work. This must be agreed by the LEA and must be given to every governor.

Governors must be over 18 years of age.

The governing body consists of the following:

- parent governors elected by the parents of children currently at the school
- teacher governors elected by the teaching staff of the school
- staff governor elected by the non-teaching staff employed at the school or under a contract for services to work at the school
- LEA governors appointed by the LEA
- co-opted governors chosen by the governors to represent the wider community; a primary school may have as an additional co-opted governor a representative of the minor authority for the area
- foundation governors appointed by the person named in the Instrument of Government (often a trustee or religious body)
- the headteacher may choose whether or not to be a governor.

No one can be a governor who has been declared bankrupt, been removed from office by charity trustees, received a prison sentence of three months or more in the previous five years, of two and a half years or more in the previous twenty years or five years at any time, or is included in the list of teachers held by the DfEE of teachers or workers who may not work with children or young people (List 99).

All governors are entitled to serve a four year term in office. Foundation governors may be required to serve a shorter term than this. Parent governors whose children leave the school during their term of office may continue to the end of the four years but teachers who leave the school must resign from the governing body. A governor can stand for subsequent terms of office if elected, appointed or co-opted again.

A governor can be disqualified if he or she persistently fails to attend meetings for a continuous period of six months.

Every governing body must have a clerk who is not a governor who is responsible for minuting meetings. The minutes must be signed by the chair.

A governing body must meet once every term. In practice most governing bodies meet either as a body or in committees much more frequently than this.

The chair of the governing body and vice-chair and chairs of committees must be elected annually at the first meeting in the school year. If the chair is absent the vice-chair takes his or her place but if the chair resigns during the year, the vice-chair does not automatically take over. There must be a fresh election. No one employed at the school may be a chair-person. The chair of governors has power to deal with any function of the governing body in an emergency and report this to the next meeting of the full body.

Notice of meetings and the agenda must be given to members seven full days in advance of the meeting. Any three governors may ask for a meeting to be called. The headteacher is entitled to attend meetings whether or not he or she has chosen to be a governor. The headteacher is also entitled to attend all committee meetings.

Decisions of the governing body and committees are made when necessary by majority vote, with the chair having a casting vote.

A quorum of the governing body is either three members or one-third of the total membership (rounded up to a whole number) whichever is the greater. The quorum must be two-thirds of the members when the governing body is dealing with the co-option of new members, the membership of headteacher and deputy headteacher selection panels, the appointment of a committee with delegated functions or the removal of the chair. Co-opted governors may not vote in any choice of other co-opted governors.

Governors may not vote in any decision in which they have a special interest. For example, the school might be deciding on a contractor to carry out work at the school and a member might be a senior employee, director of a company or a close relative to someone in a company tendering for the work.

The governing body may set up committees to deal with such matters as finance, premises, curriculum and so on. Committees must have at least three members but may co-opt non-members who have particular expertise. Non-members may vote only if this is agreed by the whole governing body and governor members must be in the majority when decisions are made. Committees may make decisions but the decisions about the following have to be made by the full governing body:

- the final choice of headteacher or deputy headteacher
- the curriculum including religious education
- matters relating to school admissions
- policy on charging for school activities
- the co-option and appointment of governors
- the provision of information to parents and approval of the annual report to parents
- the statement about pupil discipline or behaviour policy.

Minutes should be kept for all committee meetings.

There are four statutory committees which must be in place. These are the Staff Dismissal Committee, the Dismissal Appeals Committee, the Pupil Discipline Committee and the Admissions Committee. Governors must appoint someone to clerk these committees, which may be the clerk to the governing body or another person but must not be the headteacher or another governor. It may be that these functions can be combined with the work of committees with a wider remit. However, it is necessary in dealing with permanent exclusion and dismissal cases to have governors who can form an appeals committee, who have not been involved in any way with the case. Governors may therefore wish to form a first pool of members who can be called on to deal with the hearing of a pupil discipline issue and a second pool to deal with any appeals against the original decision. Similar arrangements are needed where staff discipline and dismissal are concerned.

The governing body appoints the headteacher, deputy headteacher(s) and other staff but may delegate the process of making a recommendation for appointment to a subcommittee. The appointment of the headteacher and deputies must then be ratified by the full governing body. In the case of other staff, appointments may be made by a subcommittee.

The whole governing body must approve the school budget plan and the school prospectus.

No one may be a governor of more than two schools.

Any governor who fails to attend meetings for a continuous period of six months may be disqualified from continuing to hold office as a governor of the school.

Governors should have a general complaints procedure and a complaints procedure for curriculum matters.

The responsibilities of central and local government

The Secretary of State for Education is responsible for:

- establishing and keeping under review the National Curriculum
- approval of the provision and closure of schools
- approval of the character of schools e.g. foundation, community
- determining the standards for school buildings
- approval of schemes of local financial management for schools
- providing for initial teacher training
- providing for the inspection of schools
- seeing that local education authorities provide an adequate system of education for their areas.

The local education authority is responsible for:

- providing schools which give all children in their area appropriate educational opportunities
- ensuring that the National Curriculum is implemented
- establishing schemes for local financial management of schools
- supporting schools which are in difficulties

- appointing governors to represent the local authority
- publishing admission arrangements for schools
- ensuring that pupils attend school regularly.

The structure of schooling

School is compulsory for children between the ages of 5 and 16. Maintained schools are divided into community schools, which are the responsibility of the LEA, voluntary controlled schools, which are church foundations administered by the LEA, foundation schools, which are the former grant-maintained schools but have now reverted to being an LEA responsibility, voluntary aided schools, which are normally church foundations but are partly financed by the LEA and special schools catering for pupils with special educational needs. A foundation school will employ its own staff, own its land and buildings, be able to determine the dates of the school year and the times of day it is open, be the admissions authority and be able to enter into contracts including contracts of employment. In a community school and a voluntary controlled school, these tasks will be the responsibility of the LEA.

In voluntary aided schools all buildings and repair costs are shared between the voluntary body and the LEA. In voluntary controlled schools the responsibility for premises rests with the LEA.

Schools are divided into infant schools for 5 to 7 year olds, junior schools for 7 to 11 year olds and secondary schools for 11 to 16 year olds or 11 to 18 year olds. In some areas infant and junior schools are combined to form primary schools. There are also some local authorities where first schools cater for 5 to 8 or 5 to 9 year olds and middle schools for 9 to 12 or 13 year olds.

The year group numbers are as follows:

under fives	Year R	Reception, infants, first school or primary
5–6 year olds	Year 1	Infants, first school or primary
6–7 year olds	Year 2	Infants, first school or primary
7–8 year olds	Year 3	Infants, first school or primary
8–9 year olds	Year 4	Juniors, first or middle school or primary
9–10 year olds	Year 5	Juniors, middle school or primary
10–11 year olds	Year 6	Juniors, middle school or primary
11–12 year olds	Year 7	Secondary or middle school
12–13 year olds	Year 8	Secondary or middle school
13–14 year olds	Year 9	Secondary school
14–15 year olds	Year 10	Secondary school
15–16 year olds	Year 11	Secondary school
16–17 year olds	Year 12	Secondary school sixth form
17–18 year olds	Year 13	Secondary school sixth form

Schools must meet for at least 380 half-day sessions in each school year. The school day should be divided into two sessions with a break between them. The Secretary of State recommends the following weekly lengths of lesson time for pupils:

- twenty-one hours for pupils aged 5 to 7 years
- twenty-three and a half hours for pupils aged 8 to 11 years
- twenty-four hours for pupils aged 12 to 16 years

Teachers are required to work 1,295 hours a year. In practice many teachers work far more hours than this.

Knowledge of the school

Governors need background information about their school, such as the following:

- The history of the school, when it first opened and any changes that have been made in its organisation.
- The nature of the catchment area and the particular problems this may pose. For example, a school may have a constantly changing population or large numbers of children whose first language is not English and these characteristics will create problems for the teachers.
- The size of the school, the numbers on roll and whether these are rising or falling or remaining constant. The extent to which parents are making the school their first choice. The numbers of staff and pupil–teacher ratio (PTR).
- The overall organisation of the school. How are classes made up? Is there setting by ability for any part of the curriculum? What is the management structure?
- The aims and objectives of the school.
- The financial resources of the school and their allocation.
- What are the school policies, particularly on such areas as behaviour, equal opportunities, sex education, collective worship, special educational needs?
- What extracurricular activities does the school offer? Are there any educational visits?
- What is the state of the equipment, premises and grounds?
- What are the examination/test results like? How do they compare with those from comparable schools, particularly those in the area?

The curriculum

Governors are responsible for the school curriculum. This means seeing that the National Curriculum and religious education are taught, taking account of any statement the local education authority has made on curriculum and, in primary schools, deciding whether sex education shall be taught. In secondary schools sex education is compulsory but governors need a policy about it at both levels.

The National Curriculum was made law by the Education Reform Act in 1988. Its introduction into schools was completed in 1997.

The curriculum consists of three core subjects – English, mathematics and science plus Welsh for schools in Wales – together with nine foundation subjects – art, citizenship (non-statutory at the primary stage), design and technology, history, geography, information and communication technology (ICT), a modern foreign language (MFL) (in secondary schools), music and physical education (PE).

There is also non-statutory provision for personal, social and health education (PSHE) at all stages. Religious education (RE) was already a legal requirement when the National Curriculum was introduced.

Each subject was made the province of a working party of people expert in that field who produced a report on which the curriculum was based. The original versions of the National Curriculum tended to be overloaded and a revised version was produced in 1995 with a further revision in 1999.

The National Curriculum is organised in four Key Stages as follows:

Key Stage 1	6–7 year olds	English, mathematics, science, art, design and technology, geography, history, ICT, music, physical education
Key Stage 2	8–11 year olds	As Key Stage 1
Key Stage 3	12–14 year olds	As at Key Stages 1 and 2 plus citizenship and a modern foreign language
Key Stage 4	15–16 year olds	English, mathematics, science, citizenship, design and technology, ICT, physical education and a modern foreign language

Technology, religious education and a foreign language may be short courses at Key Stage 4.

In Wales, Welsh is part of the National Curriculum at all stages. English, mathematics and science must be studied throughout schooling.

The more limited range of compulsory subjects at Key Stage 4 allows students some choice. They can continue to take art, music, history and geography or take a second foreign language, three separate sciences or combined science or any other course that the school wishes to offer. Some schools are considering vocational courses at this stage. Information and communication technology may be taught as a separate subject as well as being part of the work in other subjects.

Governors are required to have a curriculum policy which takes account of the LEA policy. The policy will determine issues such as the choices available at Key Stage 4.

Governors of primary schools may determine whether sex education in addition to the work on reproduction in the National Curriculum shall be part of the curriculum.

Religious education and the act of worship

Governors are responsible for seeing that religious education is taught in local education authority schools according to the authority's Agreed Syllabus which is the responsibility of a local Standing Advisory Committee for Religious Education (SACRE). This is a group brought together by the local authority and represents the Church of England, other religious groups in the area and teachers' organisations as well as the local authority. Church schools follow the syllabus laid down by their trust deed.

Governors are also responsible for seeing that there is a daily act of worship involving all pupils which must be broadly Christian in nature. This need not necessarily be for the whole school at the same time, which might be difficult for some schools. Pupils can be grouped according to their year groups or Key Stage groups. Acts of worship can take place at any time during the school day. Where there is a high proportion of pupils of other religions the school can apply to the local SACRE for the requirement that the assembly should be broadly Christian to be lifted. They can be grouped according to religion only if the SACRE has agreed this.

Parents have the right to withdraw their children from religious education and collective worship and from sex education but the school remains responsible for their health and safety and must make arrangements for their supervision. Teachers have a right not to take part in collective worship unless their contract of employment states otherwise.

Assessment, tests and examinations

Since September 1998 teachers must make a 'baseline' assessment of pupils within the first seven weeks of their entering school for the first time. This is intended to give teachers information about what the child has already learned and can do so that work can build on this. Governing bodies must adopt an accredited baseline assessment scheme chosen by the headteacher. Baseline assessments are likely to cover six areas of learning: language and literacy, mathematics, personal and social development, knowledge and understanding of the world, physical development and creative development.

There are national assessment tests in English, mathematics and science at the end of each of the Key Stages plus teacher assessment. At Key Stage 3 there is teacher assessment in all subjects. The tests are known as Standard Assessment Tasks (SATs) and are set nationally and marked externally. Assessment at the end of Key Stage 4 is the General Certificate of Secondary Education (GCSE). Pupils are graded in the SATs tests at one of eight levels. Pupils at Key Stage 1 are typically expected to achieve level 2 in each subject. At Key Stage 2 they are expected to achieve level 4 and at Key Stage 3 levels 5 or 6. Each pupil's SATs results must be communicated to parents together with information about comparative results of pupils of the same age in the school and nationally. The results of SATs at Key Stages 2 and 3 and GCSE are published nationally school by school.

At sixth-form level students may be taking Advanced levels (A levels) or Advanced Subsidiary levels (AS levels). Most students take two or three A levels and occasionally four. There has been a good deal of concern about the fact that English students at this stage take fewer subjects than their continental counterparts and there have been many moves to broaden the curriculum for sixth-formers. AS levels are one of these moves. AS levels are equivalent to half an A level and the idea is that students should take some AS levels alongside full A levels. A levels can also be taken in modules.

Some sixth-form students take General National Vocational Qualifications (GNVQ). These students follow a course with a vocational bias.

The headteacher must see that all the information about each pupil's progress is gathered systematically and recorded and passed from teacher to teacher. Parents have a right to see these records. Secondary schools must supply school leavers with a record of achievement which records their achievements during the time they have been at the school. This is developed by the students themselves as they move through the school and may include achievements outside the school. The record of achievement may be used to inform prospective employers or tutors in further or higher education.

Provision for pupils with special educational needs

In 1994 a Code of Practice for pupils with special needs was published (DfEE 1994b). This sets out what schools are expected to do in order to provide for pupils with special educational needs (SEN). The following responsibilities are set out for governors, who should

- do their best to secure that the necessary provision is made for any pupils who have special educational needs
- secure that the teachers in the school are aware of the importance of identifying, and providing for, those pupils who have special educational needs
- consult the LEA and the governing bodies of other schools when it seems to them necessary or desirable in the interests of coordinated special educational provision in the area as a whole
- report annually to parents on the school's policy for pupils with special educational needs
- ensure that the pupils join in the activities of the school together with pupils who do not have special educational needs, so far as that is reasonably practical and compatible with the pupils receiving the necessary special educational provision, the efficient education of other children in the school and the efficient use of resources
- have regard to this Code of Practice when carrying out their duty toward all pupils with special educational needs.

                                                            (DfEE 1994b: 6 para 2.6)

The governing body should, in cooperation with the headteacher, determine the school's general policy and approach for pupils with special educational needs, establish the appropriate staffing and funding arrangements and maintain a general oversight of the school's work.

The governing body may appoint a committee to take a particular interest in and closely monitor the school's work on behalf of pupils with special educational needs.

Each school should appoint a teacher as coordinator for work with pupils with special educational needs (known as the SENCO – special educational needs coordinator). He or she will work closely with other teachers and be responsible for the implementation of the special educational needs policy.

All teaching staff should be involved in the implementation of the policy and be fully aware of the school's procedures for identifying, assessing and making provision for these pupils.

Each school is required to keep a register of pupils with special educational needs. Maintaining this register is the responsibility of the SENCO.

Parents and the pupils concerned should be involved in decisions about provision and the parents should be kept informed of progress.

The programme for pupils with special educational needs is in several stages:

1   Initially the pupil's form or class teacher notes that he or she has special needs and informs the coordinator, who registers the pupil. Teachers should then make provision for the pupil in the normal classroom situation.

2   If there is insufficient progress after provision within the classroom, the SENCO collects relevant information, informs the pupil's parents and the headteacher and draws up an Individual Education Plan (IEP) for the pupil in consultation with him or her. Progress with this is monitored and review dates are set.

3   If there is insufficient progress with the IEP, specialists, such as educational psychologists or advisory teachers from outside the school, are involved in analysing the problems and helping to draw up another individual education plan. Parents and the pupil are involved in this. Progress is again monitored and review dates set.

4   If there is still insufficient progress, consideration will be given to a statutory assessment of special educational needs. This is the responsibility of the LEA, which must inform the parents about the procedures, the name of the officer concerned and their right to make representations and submit written evidence within a given time limit. If the LEA, having looked at the evidence, decides there is a case for making an assessment, it must seek educational, medical, psychological and social service advice together with any other advice which appears to be relevant.

5   The assessment may result in a Statement of Special Educational Needs. This states the provision which needs to be made for the pupil. This may involve particular kinds of help, specific equipment, or a move to a specialist school or unit. The Statement carries with it resources for provision for the pupil in question. It also requires regular review.

Questions to consider

1   What arrangements have we to enable new governors to gain the knowledge they need to work effectively?

2   Governors are responsible for seeing that the National Curriculum and religious education are taught. How do we know that this is happening?

3   Is the school complying with the law which requires a daily act of worship which is broadly Christian in character?

4   What record-keeping system is the school employing?

5   What provision is the school making for pupils with special educational needs?

6   Are pupils with special educational needs included in all the activities which the school offers?

Chapter 3

Roles and responsibilities of governors

Governors are there to support the headteacher and staff and to provide a range of additional expertise. They have overall responsibility for the conduct of the school while the head and senior staff have responsibility for its day-to-day running and management. *School Governors: A Guide to the Law* (DfEE 1997) describes the relationship between the head and the governing body as follows:

> The governing body have a general responsibility for seeing that the school is run effectively, acting within the framework set by legislation and the policies of the LEA, so that it provides the best possible education for its pupils. But they are not expected to take detailed decisions about the day-to-day management of the school – that is the job of the head. A good head will discuss all aspects of school life with the governing body.
>
> (DfEE 1997: 15)

Governors' roles

Governors might be said to have five main roles.

Strategic or steering role

Governors set a framework for executive decisions taken by the headteacher. They steer the school to some extent.

Executive role

There are, however, occasions when they take executive decisions such as when they deal with appeals and grievances, or exclusions. The most important executive decisions are made in the appointment of the headteacher and deputies.

Monitoring role

Governors need to check that their decisions and policies are being implemented and that monitoring is going on at all levels in the school.

Critical friend role

Governors need to be able to ask challenging questions of the headteacher and staff of the school and to provide both pressure and support. It is also important that governors offer praise whenever possible.

Accountability

The governing body of a school provides public accountability for the spending of public money.

Governors' responsibilities

The governing body holds its authority as a group for decisions. Individual governors have no powers of their own. Governors' responsibilities might be said to include the following areas.

Helping to formulate and agree the aims and objectives of the school and reviewing how far they are being achieved

The formulation of aims and objectives needs to be a joint effort by head, staff and governors with some consultation of parents and perhaps pupils, especially in secondary schools. It is not enough simply to state aims and objectives. They need to be brought to the attention of parents and pupils probably at the beginning of each school year and reviewed regularly by governors.

Ensuring that the school prospectus is published annually

The prospectus should contain the following information:

- Name, address, telephone and fax numbers of the school.
- Type of school: infant, junior, secondary, special, middle, selective or non-selective, single-sex or mixed.
- Details of school hours and the terms and holidays in the school year.
- The names of the headteacher and the chair of governors.
- The names and responsibilities of the teaching staff.
- The names and responsibilities of the non-teaching staff.
- A plan of the school.
- A statement of the school admissions policy.
- A statement of the school's beliefs and values and its aims and objectives.
- Details of the curriculum for different age groups and how the teaching is organised.
- A summary of the charging and remissions policy.
- Details of the religious education programme and a reminder that parents can withdraw their children from this subject and from assembly if they wish.
- Information about any affiliation to a particular religion or religious denomination.

- The school's policy on sex education and the parents' right to withdraw a child from any sex education programme except that which is part of the National Curriculum.
- Details of the arrangements for meeting special educational needs.
- Information about the school's National Curriculum assessment results with comparative information about national results.
- Arrangements for making complaints about the curriculum.
- A statement of school rules and disciplinary procedures.
- Information about pupil absence rates.
- Information about uniform.
- Information about home–school links.
- A statement about homework policy.
- A description of arrangements for the pastoral care of pupils.

Secondary schools need to provide in addition:

- Details of examination results with comparative information about local and national results.
- Details of the careers' education and work experience offered.
- Information about school leavers' destinations.

Monitoring the work of the school

Governors are responsible for the overall conduct of the school. This means that they need to monitor what is happening and find ways of keeping in touch with the teaching and learning which is taking place. Some of the research into the work of governing bodies suggests that teaching and learning are not discussed at meetings as often as more mundane matters.

Making, ratifying and reviewing policies

Some policies may be made by governors; others will be a joint effort between the head and staff on the one hand and the governors on the other. Yet others may be formulated by the head and staff, discussed and agreed by governors. Governors are legally required to have policies or statements about

- procedures for admission and appeals
- aims and objectives of the school
- attendance, behaviour and pupil conduct
- charging and remissions for school activities, such as visits
- child protection
- complaints
- curriculum
- discipline of pupils including steps to prevent all forms of bullying
- employment – involving staff discipline, pay, competence and grievances
- health education
- pupil records and reports
- religious education and collective worship

- sex education
- special needs.

Overseeing the school's finances

Under the scheme for local management of schools (LMS) the head and governors have responsibility for deciding how to spend the money available for staff, other resources, premises and other needs. Technology has made this task somewhat easier in that it is possible to obtain regular information about how spending is going. Governors must make sure that the school keeps within the budget and provides regular and accurate records of expenditure and income.

Overseeing the state of the premises, equipment and grounds

Governors need to keep the premises under review and make sure that the LEA in the case of community and controlled schools is aware of any problems.

Overseeing the curriculum and the teaching and learning programme

Governors are responsible for seeing that the National Curriculum is taught and for making decisions about any choices which this allows. This is a responsibility which many governors find difficult, feeling that they do not know enough about what should be taught. However, it is important that governors do everything possible to find out what is going on by visiting the school, studying examination and test results and hearing from teachers about how they are working. In considering the curriculum and making a curriculum policy, governors in other than voluntary schools are required to have regard to the LEA's curriculum policy. They must also consider what arrangements are to be made for pupils with special educational needs.

Ensuring that religious education is taught and that there is daily collective worship

Religious education should be taught according to the Agreed Syllabus of the local authority or the syllabus of the school's trust deed in the case of voluntary schools. Parents may withdraw their children from both religious education and collective worship if they wish but the school is still responsible for them.

Ensuring that good provision is made for pupils with special educational needs

Governors need to be kept informed of how many pupils are on the register of pupils with special needs and of the provision which is being made for them. They should also be concerned with provision for any pupils with exceptional ability. It is a good idea for one governor to be especially concerned with these pupils.

Working with the head and staff to formulate the School Development Plan

Schools are required to produce a school development plan (SDP) covering about three years at a time and update it annually. Making the plan means setting priorities and working out how they are to be achieved.

Dealing with the appointment, development, pay and discipline of staff

Governors are responsible for appointing the headteacher and deputy headteacher(s); they may delegate the interviewing of candidates to a subcommittee but these appointments must be ratified by the full governing body. They are also responsible for the appointment of other staff but may delegate this to the headteacher or a subcommittee. Staff discipline is also a responsibility of the governing body. Staff pay should be reviewed annually. In the case of the headteacher and deputy headteacher(s) increases in pay may be made if previously agreed targets have been achieved. Governors are also responsible for seeing that staff have the opportunity to develop their work through attendance at in-service courses and through the use of the school's in-service days.

Ensuring that there is good discipline in the school

Governors need to have a behaviour policy which sets out the requirements for pupils' behaviour. They should also be informed about any exclusions and will be involved in making the decision where these are permanent. There is evidence nationally that black boys of Caribbean origin are more likely to be excluded than other pupils. Governors should be aware of any particular groups of pupils who are over-represented in this aspect of discipline or any other. Governors also need to be kept informed of truancy figures.

Seeing that there are equal opportunities for pupils of both sexes, ethnic minority groups, different social classes and pupils with disabilities

Governors should have an equal opportunities policy which sets out the way in which the school should treat different groups of pupils to ensure that they have equal opportunities of getting a good education. They should also be aware of any differences in performance between different groups of pupils and encourage work to improve the performance of weaker groups. Reports on examination and test results should include information about the performance of different groups of pupils, particularly boys and girls.

Receiving and acting upon inspection reports

Schools are inspected at five to six yearly intervals and once the report is received, governors with the headteacher and staff are responsible for drawing up an action plan.

Setting annual targets for the school

Governors are required to set targets for the achievement of pupils each year and make these available to parents. They are required to set and publish the following targets:

- percentage of pupils attaining level 4 or above in English at Key Stage 2
- percentage of pupils attaining level 4 or above in mathematics at Key Stage 2
- percentage of pupils attaining five or more GCSEs or equivalent grades A*–C
- percentage of pupils attaining one or more GCSEs or equivalent grades A*–G
- average GCSE (or equivalent) points score for each pupil.

Other targets can also be set such as a target to improve attendance and punctuality, increase involvement in extracurricular activities, increase links between the school and the local community or to limit the number of pupils excluded during a school year. Staff will need to give a good deal of thought to this, selecting targets which are achievable with hard work on behalf of everyone concerned.

LEAs are also required to set targets based on those set by their schools. Their plan must show the priorities for improvement, how the programme is derived from audits and national priorities and how it will contribute to achieving listed targets and how the activities in the plan will give support to schools causing concern.

Providing an annual report to parents on the work of the governing body

The annual report should be discussed at an annual meeting of parents. Many schools have found this requirement difficult in that parents tend not to attend these meetings in any number. It helps if the meeting can include something which attracts parents such as an opportunity to look at pupils' work or an exhibition or concert for part of the meeting.

Providing a home–school agreement

From September 1999 all schools must have in place a home–school agreement, normally signed by parents, a representative of the school and, where appropriate, the pupil.

Marketing the school to the local community

Schools depend for their finances on attracting pupils. It is therefore essential that a school consider how to market itself to the community.

Developing the skills of governors in order to give good support for the school

Local authorities provide training for governors and members of the governing body should be encouraged to take advantage of these opportunities. A governing body can also profitably take time to consider how successfully it is working.

Division of responsibilities between the headteacher and the governing body

The *School Governor's Manual* (Croner 1999: 1–103) sets out these responsibilities (see Table 3.1).

Table 3.1 Responsibilities of governing body and headteacher

	Governing body	Headteacher
	The governing body and head agree the aims, values, ethos priorities of the school. These will be identified in the school development plan.	
Planning	determines curriculum policy in consultation with the head	draws up school curriculum plan, including any legal requirements
	encourages governors to show an interest in specific curriculum areas	ensures detailed implementation of curriculum
	ensures the delivery of the curriculum	
	draws up policy for special educational needs	implements policy for SEN and oversees the application of the Code of Practice
Pastoral	draws up behaviour policy and complaints procedure	promulgates rules and disciplinary measures and exercises power to exclude pupils
	draws up home–school agreements	
Staffing	determines staffing complement	draws up staffing plan
	determines procedure for appointing staff and participates accordingly	selects staff within the limits of delegation agreed by the governing body
	adjudicates on personnel issues referred to it	manages staff and handles personnel issues
Marketing/ promotion	approves marketing plan	devises marketing approach that does not denigrate other schools
Premises	receives regular reports on inspections	ensures regular inspections are carried out
Charging	determines policy for charging for school activities	implements policy for charging
Finance	approves budget	draws up budget
	agrees limits of delegation and virement	incurs expenditure within delegated limits

Questions to consider

1   Have we agreed the aims of the school? Do we need to reconsider them from time to time?
2   Does our prospectus cover all the ground it is supposed to?
3   Are we making provision for pupils who have exceptional ability as well as those with other special educational needs? Have we a governor who is specially concerned with these pupils?
4   In what ways are we involved with the school development plan?
5   What targets have we set for the school? How shall we know whether they have been achieved?

Chapter 4

Working as a team

A good governing body needs to be a team in which all members contribute to its work. Creese (1995: 18) suggests that the following benefits ensue from good team work:

- help and support for team members
- increased commitment from team members and a sense of 'belonging'
- improved communication and coordination
- opportunities for team members to learn from one another
- increased enjoyment and satisfaction for the team members.

The effective team

The governors of St Peter's school decided that they needed to spend some time thinking about where the school was going in the future. They agreed to spend a Saturday discussing their vision for the future and its implications for the aims of the school which they had worked out some years ago.

They started off working in small groups with the brief of setting out what they would like to see if they visited the school in three years' time. The groups then reported back to the whole governing body. This gave rise to some lively discussion because some people wanted the school to be more formal in its approaches and others were opposed to this view. Gradually people came together to find a view on which they could agree and it was decided that a small group of volunteers would meet and put the views expressed into a document which they could use as a plan for the future.

The discussion led on to a discussion of the values they each held about education and they decided that these too needed to be agreed and set down for future reference.

The day included a cold buffet lunch arranged by two of the members and it was felt that this social occasion contributed to the feeling of being a team.

Once the statements about vision and values had been drawn up, the governors met with the staff to discuss them further with the idea that they might be modified or added to in the light of the views of the teachers. The school's aims and objectives were then reviewed in the light of this work and a mission statement was agreed.

Once a school has agreed vision and values and aims and objectives these need to be regularly reviewed and it is a good idea to put it on the agenda for a governors' meeting each year.

A governing body and the staff of a school need shared aims and values. These may be difficult to achieve for the governors because there may be some who have become governors because they disagree with the philosophy and values that the staff appear to represent and others who have become governors because they strongly support the school's values. Talking through the problems may help to move members nearer to a consensus.

Effectiveness and the feeling of being a team will also come from other occasions when the governors set aside time to discuss issues important for the school. Such meetings can give a sense of 'togetherness' especially if they include a meal taken together. Training days for the whole team can also be valuable in bringing people together.

An effective governing body has good communication. The clerk to the governors is in an important role here in seeing that people are given all the papers needed for each meeting and any useful information, such as newsletters to parents, or material from the local authority or central government which may come in between meetings.

An effective governing body has good relationships with the school staff. In a primary school where the staff tends to be smaller, it may be possible on a number of occasions for staff and governors to work together on planning for the school. For example, there may be joint discussion to arrive at the school's vision for the future or about the school development plan when it is in its early stages, or staff and governors may talk together about the school's relationships with its parents. In most secondary schools and in larger primary schools this would be difficult to do and governors may work with small groups of staff from time to time. Governors visits to see the school at work and having link governors with departments or classes may also help to foster good relationships and there may be some social occasions when governors and staff meet together.

Leadership

An effective team needs good leadership. This should come in the main from the chair but there will also be occasions when the headteacher is leading and other occasions when the chair of one of the committees or someone with specialist knowledge in a particular area takes the lead. Leadership of a group requires the leader to see that every member has a chance to contribute. The leader needs to sum up the findings of the group at intervals and move them on to conclusions when this is appropriate. A good leader consults and seeks consensus and enables members of the group to talk through their differences.

Baginsky *et al.* (1991) studied the work of the governing body in forty-three schools, twenty-one primary, twenty secondary and two special. They found that the chairs saw themselves very much in the leadership role. They felt that it was their job to be available to advise, support and listen to the head and be on the spot to help to solve problems. One chair described his role as follows:

My job is to ensure that the education of the children is delivered to the highest standard and in the most cost effective manner, and to be responsible to the parents for ensuring that delivery takes place.

(Baginsky et al. 1991: 23)

They found some cases where the headteacher and chair of governors were at odds and felt that it was important to clarify their respective roles, which should be complementary. It may be worthwhile taking time to set out the respective roles of the chair and the headteacher. The chair's role is to lead the team, build consensus, involve and support all governors. He or she should support the headteacher and senior management team, act as a critical friend of the headteacher, ensure that the school has developed appropriate policies, boost staff morale. The head's role is to act as the leading professional, see that the school has a clear vision of where it is going which is shared with the governors and staff, manage change, build a staff team, manage the interface with the governors and with parents, sustain staff morale and act as professional adviser to the governing body. The head should ensure that governors have sufficient information about the life and work of the school to fulfil their role.

The chair has no specific right to make decisions on behalf of the governors but there may be emergency situations in which he or she will have to make such a decision which should be reported to the full governing body at the first possible opportunity.

Committee structure

All governing bodies need to have committees because the amount of work involved in being a governor is too great to be confined to meetings of the whole group. Berkshire Education Department (1997: 1) set out the following reasons for having committees. Committees will:

1   Ease the workload of the full governing body.
2   Provide opportunities for issues to be debated at length, in detail.
3   Provide opportunities for governors to develop skills and knowledge in specific areas and therefore enable discussion to take place at an informed level.
4   Provide the school with the opportunity to strengthen the partnership between the staff and the governors. Committees can have members who are not governors, so enabling people with expertise to be involved in, and inform discussion. Non-governors are not able to vote.
5   Share the workload of the chairman of the governing body. The committee will take on the paperwork, consultations etc. that fall within its remit so freeing the chairman of that area of work.
6   Speed up decision making.

Delegation

Some committees can have delegated powers. Others must refer back to the full governing body. A governing body may not delegate decisions about the following although committees may discuss such items and recommend decisions to the full governing body:

- admission of pupils to the school
- appointment of co-opted governors
- matters to do with the school curriculum, including the National Curriculum and religious education
- provision for sex education
- provision of collective worship
- times of school sessions and the dates of school terms and holidays
- general principles concerning school discipline
- the charging policy for visits and other activities which are not part of the school's main curriculum
- approval of the annual report to parents.

The governing body must delegate to a committee matters relating to the dismissal of staff or the exclusion of pupils. In these cases it is necessary to have other governors who have not been party to the original decisions to act as an appeal committee.

Membership

Some governing bodies encourage their members to change their membership of committees from time to time so that they get to know all aspects of the work of the governing body. Others prefer their members to specialise.

Membership of committees will depend to some extent on governors' individual interests. It is a good idea when a new governor joins to suggest that he or she attends the meetings of any committee which seems to be of interest with a view to deciding which ones to join.

Membership of committees may be open to members of staff and others who are not governors but have particular interest in the topics under discussion. Some secondary school governing bodies also include student representatives at some of their meetings, often with a brief to report on student views on given topics, very often reporting on business at school council meetings. One pupil reported on his experience of attending governors' meetings as follows:

> My participation at the meetings is to observe and to submit a report to the governors concerning the activities of the school council during the term. I believe that pupil participation should be greater, particularly for the feedback as it is really the students who experience the positive and negative aspects of school life.
>
> The experience of attending such meetings which I see as positive are, it has given me an insight into how the school is run and who holds the ultimate decision-making power. Above all I am impressed by the dedication and hard work put in by the governing body.

Types of committees

The number of committees a governing body may have will vary according to the size of the school and the amount of work to be done. Deem *et al.* (1995) studied ten schools in two LEAs and found that the number of committees varied from two to eleven. Most schools will probably have committees dealing with curriculum, finance, pupil welfare and relationships with parents, premises, marketing/public relations, staffing/personnel, suspensions and exclusions.

Governors must by law have committees to deal with pupil discipline and appeals and with staff dismissal and appeals. The members of these committees must not have been involved in any preliminary discussion of these cases and the appeals committees must be separate from the pupil discipline and staff dismissal committees. Governors of foundation and voluntary aided schools must also have a committee which deals with admissions and sets the policy for deciding who shall be admitted to the school. In community and controlled schools, the LEA is the admissions authority.

Terms of reference

The committees will need terms of reference. These should set out clearly each committee's responsibilities and these should be reviewed regularly. The Berkshire guidance on committees suggests that these should include statements of the following:

- What constitutes a quorum? The rule for the main governing body of one-third of members rounded up is too few for committees. A possible quorum might be three voting members.
- What is the purpose of the committee and what is it intended to achieve? There may be tasks which it needs to undertake regularly.
- How is the chair chosen? The governing body as a whole may decide on the chair-person or leave it to the individual committee to elect their own chair. Governors who are employed at the school are not eligible to be appointed as chairs.
- What powers does the committee have? What can be decided by the committee and what must be referred back to the main governing body?
- What arrangements should there be for reporting back? Many governing bodies will have an agenda item at the full meeting which gives each committee a chance to report back.
- How often will the terms of reference be reviewed and by whom?

Finance committee

A finance committee might include in its terms of reference responsibility to review and agree the school's proposals for the budget and recommend it to the full governing body, to review the school fund account, to review expenditure and present progress reports to the full governing body, to identify problems and recommend changes to keep expenditure on target and to initiate action where necessary on the understanding that all decisions taken are reported back to the full governing body.

Curriculum committee

A curriculum committee might have in its terms of reference responsibility for monitoring test and examination results, monitoring the teaching of the National Curriculum, approving and reviewing the assessment policy, approving and reviewing provision for religious education and collective worship, deciding the school's policy for sex education, monitoring provision for children with special educational needs and those with exceptional ability, arrangements for school visits which involve an overnight stay and identifying curriculum requirements which have implications for the budget.

Pastoral care committee

A pastoral care committee might maintain an overview of the provision for personal and social education, including health education and for reporting and recording procedures. It might be responsible for seeing that there are equal opportunities for all pupils. It should approve and review the school's behaviour policy. It might also include the school's relationships with parents in its remit, ensuring that all relevant information is communicated to them, approving and reviewing the home–school contract and deal with complaints from parents if these have not been satisfied by the headteacher and staff.

Marketing/public relations committee

A marketing/public relations committee might be responsible for all the arrangements for the annual report to parents and the parents' meeting as well as identifying and recommending action to keep the school's image present in the locality and encouraging pupils to come to the school. It might also inform itself of parental views through questionnaires such as those suggested in the Appendix.

Staffing/personnel committee

A staffing/personnel committee might have responsibility for reviewing and agreeing the staffing provision at the school within the constraints of budgetary and curriculum requirements, dealing with all proposals for staff appointments, agreeing procedures for staff selection, reviewing and agreeing the staff appraisal procedure and monitoring its implementation, contributing to the appraisal of the headteacher, reviewing and agreeing staff training programmes and reviewing and agreeing the pay of the headteacher and deputies and the staff. It might also be concerned with any grievances which are brought by the staff and with some aspects of staff discipline. A separate committee of governors is needed for decisions to dismiss and a second committee whose members have had no dealings with the original decision will be needed to deal with appeals.

Premises committee

A premises committee might be concerned with the use of premises, grounds and facilities out of school hours by members of the community, approve and review the lettings policy, review and make recommendations on accommodation, cleaning, caretaking, internal decoration and maintenance, review and make recommendations with regard to the security and safety of premises, contents and grounds with particular regard to the Health and Safety at Work Act 1974 and other relevant legislation, agree and review the school's health and safety policy and monitor its implementation, ensure that there is an efficient use of such utilities as water, electricity, gas and oil and maintain an overview of the costs of the premises.

Pupil suspensions and exclusions committee

The committee dealing with pupil suspensions and exclusions will probably meet only when there are cases to deal with unless they have other tasks to do which require regular meetings. As in the case of staff discipline, another group of governors who have not been involved in the original decisions will be needed to act as an appeal committee when this is required. In making decisions such as the permanent exclusion of a pupil or the reinstatement of a pupil who has been excluded, governors will need to consider whether all the possible avenues to avoid exclusion have been explored, how often the pupil has been in trouble, the effect of his or her behaviour on other pupils and the problems posed for teachers. The headteacher should not be present when such decisions are made and there must be at least three governors involved.

Meetings

Baginsky et al. (1991) in studying the work of governing bodies found that:

> Efficient meetings were considered to be well-planned and well-constructed, running through crisply but not too quickly. A well-chaired meeting was concise, discussions were kept to the point and the main outcomes were summarised by the chair.
>
> (Baginsky et al. 1991: 25)

Headteachers in this study saw themselves at meetings of the governing body as there 'to advise, to guide and to provide information, in much the same way as an executive manager or chief officer' (p. 46).

The agenda

The agenda for any meeting, which must go out in time to give members seven days' notice of the meeting, should make it clear what the purpose of each item may be, whether it is for information or for decision making. It should also list any accompanying papers for each item so that members know in advance what they should be receiving. This is also helpful for the clerk in checking whether everything which should go out has been included. Members should be aware of how to get an item included in the agenda and should warn the chair if they want to raise an item under any other business. Such items should not be substantial. It is a good idea to put items which need decisions early in the agenda so that enough time can be taken to consider the issues involved. It is also helpful in planning the agenda to estimate how long each item might take. This can help to avoid having agendas which are too long and can be a useful guide to a chair.

The agenda should include apologies for absence, the minutes of the previous meeting and matters arising, the headteacher's report, committee reports, other items, any other business and the date of the next meeting.

Seating

Comfort is important at meetings since people tend to stop paying attention if they are uncomfortable. Primary schools, particularly infant schools, need to try to find enough adult-sized chairs and attention should be given to temperature. It is also a good idea to ensure that the chair-person is not seated with his or her back to the light so that looking to the chair is a strain.

It has been noted by some researchers that people who disagree with each other tend to sit on opposite sides in meetings. People who have a common axe to grind may sit together.

The chair's role

The chair's role in meetings is to see that everyone has a chance to contribute. It is often necessary to look for signs that someone wants to say something but is hesitating to do so. Deem *et al.* (1995) studied what happened at governors' meetings and found that women, members of ethnic minority groups and those working in unskilled jobs or were unemployed tended to contribute less than other members so this is something to watch out for. Teacher governors may also be hesitant about expressing their views, especially if these differ from those of the headteacher and it may be necessary to invite their opinion very specifically from time to time. Deem *et al.* (1995) found that other governors tended to be ambivalent towards teacher governors wondering whether their self-interest would allow them to make disinterested decisions.

It can sometimes be helpful when it is important that all views about a topic are aired, to break into buzz groups of two or three to discuss the topic first for a few minutes. This ensures that everyone has plenty to say when the whole group comes together again.

An important part of chairing a meeting is to sum up at intervals what has been said and in particular what has been agreed and who will act on the decision.

The clerk's role

The clerk's role is to take charge of the election of the chair, compile the agenda with the chair, send out the agenda and other papers for each meeting and any relevant papers which come between meetings, take the minutes, provide information about current rules and regulations, advise on correct procedure, write letters on behalf of the governing body, inform members of opportunities for training and (where appropriate), arrange it and keep a record of all letters and documents relevant to the governing body.

The clerk as well as the chair needs to ensure that when decisions are made it is clear who is responsible for any action following.

The headteacher's role

The headteacher attends a governors' meeting primarily in a reporting and advisory role. The headteacher's report is an important part of the meeting. Earley (1994) in a study of governing bodies found that some headteachers tended to keep their governors at arm's length wanting them to act in a rubber-stamping capacity. In such cases the headteacher's report may disguise more than it reveals and governors need to take the opportunities they can to question its content. The headteacher can make the system work or can work against it. Working with governors to ensure a proper involvement of the governors in the decision-making process is a test of the headteacher's management skills.

The headteacher is also an important source of information and advice. He or she knows the internal working of the school and how the outcomes of decisions will affect those who work in it. Where headteacher and governing body work together the outcomes are profitable for the school.

Minutes

All meetings of the governing body should be minuted and the minutes should make clear the decisions that have been taken and who is responsible for carrying them out. It is a good idea either to underline actions to be taken with the name of the person or persons responsible or to have a separate column on the right-hand side of the page for actions. Meetings of committees should be circulated to all governors. The minutes of all meetings of governors should list those present and apologies for absence.

The governing body can decide if some items should be confidential and these should be minuted separately. The rest of the minutes, agendas and any papers considered by a committee or the full governing body must be available for inspection at the school. It is a good idea for the minutes of the main governors' meeting to be available to staff.

The yearly pattern of meetings

Most governing bodies now meet twice a term with committee meetings in addition. It can be helpful if the chair and vice-chair plan the dates of meetings for all the committees so that there are no clashes of date. Each committee can then change any dates which do not suit them, knowing that they will not clash with the meetings of another committee.

It is a good idea to have a yearly programme of items which need regular discussion, such as reviewing of policies. Some of these will be items for the full meeting, others for particular committees. Items which could be programmed as occurring regularly are as follows:

- Report on test and examination results. This will usually take place in September each year.
- Review of draft budget for coming year and its finalisation. The timing of this will depend on when information is received about the money which will be available. It will probably be an item for more than one meeting.
- Any changes in curriculum proposed. This could be discussed at any time but such changes are most likely to be implemented in the Autumn term so the discussion will probably need to take place in the Spring term.
- Staffing needs for the next year. This is likely to be discussed in the Spring term following discussion about curriculum.
- The school development plan. This will need to be discussed at more than one meeting, starting with discussion about any audit needed and going on to the discuss the draft plan.
- Preparation of governors' report to parents. The timing of this will depend on when the school holds the annual meeting.
- The pay of the headteacher and deputy head(s). Governors can decide on any salary increases for the head and deputy head(s). This should depend on the meeting of previously agreed targets.

Effective meetings

Effective meetings are those in which everyone feels involved and able to contribute. The chair operates an easy control, ensuring that members know what has been decided and who will be responsible for carrying out any decisions. There is plenty of opportunity for discussion but no one is allowed to go on for too long and members are made aware of progress through short summaries at the end of each item. At the end of the meeting everyone should feel that something has been achieved and that the time has been well spent.

Questions to consider

1   Do we have a vision for the school which is shared with the staff?
2   How far are we in agreement about the values we think are important for education?
3   How good is our communication?
4   Are we clear about the respective roles of headteacher and chair?
5   Does our committee structure provide for all the matters we need to discuss?
6   Have all our committees clear terms of reference?
7   Are our meetings run satisfactorily?
8   Are there any members who say nothing at meetings? Do we know why this is? Should we do something about it?
9   Do we have a yearly pattern of meetings?

Chapter 5

Monitoring the work of the school

The effectiveness of governors must be judged by whether they make any difference to the learning of the pupils. This means that governors need to be looking for pointers to the success of the teaching and the achievement of the pupils. This is not easy, because governors are not inspectors and are not usually in a position to make judgements about the teaching and learning from observation, although this is valuable. Governors are to some extent dependent upon the information which the school is prepared to make available and their ability to question the information they are given. The programme of monitoring should perform three functions:

- establish the current situation
- assess progress in implementing plans or policies
- provide information needed as the basis for further action

In the long run the purpose of monitoring is to discover whether the actions that governors have taken have resulted in improvements in the learning of the pupils. In planning any particular action, thought should be given to the way in which its success will be judged.

There are four main sources of information available to governors to help them make judgements about their school's performance. These are:

1   Information available about the school, such as the school prospectus, headteacher's reports to governors, inspection reports, examination and test results, attendance records, progress of the school development plan and curriculum plans, financial information and newsletters to parents.
2   Information about comparable schools with similar intakes. This information is available to schools both nationally and locally.
3   Information deliberately sought by governors, such as visits to the school, observation of teaching (including shadowing a pupil or group of pupils), governor links with classes in a primary school or departments in a secondary school, attendance at school events (such as assemblies, concerts, plays and presentation evenings), inviting staff or pupils to committee meetings to discuss their work, questionnaires to pupils and parents, and attendance at parents' evenings.

4   Informal sources of information, such as the appearance of the school (including the evidence of displays and its cleanliness), reception of visitors, staff–pupil relationships, behaviour of pupils about the school (especially the behaviour of pupils at the beginning and end of school and at lunchtime, the appearance of pupils, governors' relationships with teaching and support staff, involvement with the Parent–Teacher Association (PTA), and comments from members of the community.

Information available about the school

There is usually a good deal of information available to governors which will enable them to gain some idea of how well the school is working, which may be reported to meetings or be contained in various documents.

School prospectus

Every school now has to provide a prospectus which should give the information described in Chapter 3. This will give a background to the school.

Headteacher's reports to governors

Headteachers normally give a report to the governors at each full governors' meeting. This should contain a good deal of evidence of how the school is working but it has to be remembered that a headteacher may choose to tell governors about the good things and say little about the less satisfactory ones. However, most headteachers give honest reports about the school and by asking questions governors can learn more. There is likely to be information about the following:

- Numbers of pupils in the school. This is likely to be an item at the end of term when numbers for the next term are known. It is important that governors are kept aware of numbers, since these reflect the money which will be available to the school in the coming year. Falling numbers in an area which does not have a declining population may indicate a need for better marketing of the school.
- Information about staff. Some may be leaving for other posts or retiring or going on maternity leave or have been absent through illness. There may be new appointments or promotions. Some staff will have spent time at in-service courses. There may have been problems with staff which should be reported.
- Information about pupils. This may include information about exclusions and the reasons for them. Governors need to be aware of how many exclusions there are and consider whether enough effort has been made to avoid them. There may also be pupils who have done exceptionally well in some activity.
- Information about the curriculum. Changes in the curriculum need to be discussed by governors but a headteacher may report on ways in which staff are developing work or on difficulties being experienced in making particular provision.

- Updating about the progress of the school development plan and any action plan following an inspection.
- Information about administrative issues. There may be changes in the school day, changes in the responsibilities of particular members of staff or changes in organisation.
- Information about the school premises. There may be plans for rooms to be redecorated or refurbished. Cleaning may be causing problems. Heating may be unsatisfactory and so on. Information about health and safety issues and security may be included.
- Information about relationships with parents and any plans for meeting parents.

Some of these issues may be dealt with by individual committees.

Inspection reports

The Education (Schools) Act 1992 brought in new arrangements for the inspection of schools starting in September 1993. The arrangements for inspection were made the responsibility of the Office for Standards in Education (Ofsted) which would organise a programme of inspections by independently operating teams, each led by a registered inspector. The teams must include a lay person who has not been professionally involved with education and all members will have undergone special training. The registered inspector will have had additional training and will be responsible for recruiting a team for each inspection, providing the school with a list of the inspection team, the conduct of the inspection and the production of the final report. Inspections are governed by an inspection framework so that the same things are looked for in all schools.

The overall purpose of inspections is to give information to governors and parents about the work of the school, to provide schools with an evaluation of their performance, to identify schools which are failing and to gather evidence about national trends in the education system as a whole. The inspection report is a very important source of information for governors.

The inspection framework was modified as from January 2000 and now includes provision for short inspections for the most effective schools, judged on:

- a favourable report from the last inspection
- a record of improvement (or sustained high standards)
- favourable achievements in relation to similar schools
- good overall performance in relation to national averages.

A short inspection will lead to a summary report commenting on what the school does well and where it could improve and a list of what the school should do to improve further. The short inspection is intended as a health check on good schools. If such an inspection exposes weaknesses then a full inspection will follow. In the short inspection not all teachers will be seen teaching. A full inspection will involve a larger team of inspectors and give a full evaluation of the areas of learning, subjects, courses and other features inspected and a list of what the school could do to improve further.

Originally schools were to be inspected every four years. This has now been changed to five to six years for the most effective schools and four to five years for the rest.

The registered inspector will give the school advance notice of the inspection and detailed information about the team of inspectors. For a full inspection they are likely to spend at least a week in all but the smallest schools and will see all members of staff at work. Teacher performance is graded and information about individual teachers is given to the headteacher in confidence. A questionnaire is sent to parents asking for their views of the school and a special parents' meeting is held with the registered inspector at which parents may express their views. Their comments are confidential to the inspector but the consensus of views will be shared with the headteacher. The registered inspector will also meet the chair of governors and the chair of the finance committee.

The inspectors will look at attendance, at the standards achieved by the pupils bearing in mind their ability, at their response in lessons and their behaviour and discipline about the school. Spiritual and moral development will be assessed, equal opportunities and provision for pupils with special educational needs. They will also look at the overall efficiency and effectiveness of the management and administration of the school, at planning and at the policies which have been developed and the extent to which they are carried out and at staff development, the work of the governors and governor training.

At the end of the inspection, the registered inspector will meet the governors to give a verbal report on the main findings and answer any questions. The written report and a summary of it must follow within five weeks. Copies of the report must be sent to the governing body, which must send a copy of the summary to all parents. The report must be made publicly available to any member of the public who wishes to see it. The governing body must provide anyone who asks with a copy of the report, and may charge for reproduction of the report if they wish. The Department for Education advises that copies should be sent to the press and to the local public library, although this not statutory.

The governors must then draw up an action plan within forty working days of receiving the report. The action plan must address the key issues raised by the inspectors, state the action proposed, who is responsible for it, the time scale and criteria for evaluation. Where possible this should be incorporated into the school development plan. A copy of the action plan must be sent to all parents, all employees of the school, Ofsted and the LEA and those who appoint foundation governors. Governors should then give a report on progress with the action plan at the annual parents' meeting.

Some schools will fail their inspection. When this happens they are put on 'special measures'. Both the DfEE and Ofsted will write to the governors and the LEA giving guidance on the action required. The governing body, in consultation with the LEA, will draw up its action plan and progress towards it is monitored by the LEA. The LEA must also submit to the DfEE its own commentary and statement of action. The Diocese may also be involved when church schools come into this category. There will be a monitoring visit by Her Majesty's Inspectors (HMI) about six months after the original inspection and they will make a judgement about progress and advise on areas of weakness in the action plans. They will then visit the school once a term or more frequently if this is judged to be necessary. When HMI believe that the school no longer requires special measures a further inspection is made and if they are satisfied a report will be produced saying this. If progress is not made the school may be closed and reopened as a new school on the same site with appropriate changes of staff.

A school may not be considered failing to the extent of being placed on special measures but may be found to have serious weaknesses. The LEA and governors and where relevant, the Diocesan Board, must make an action plan to remedy the weaknesses within a year of receiving the inspection report. The LEA will work with the school to achieve progress.

The inspection report is one of the most important pieces of information for governors. While not all schools are satisfied that their report truly reflects the work of the school, it is the nearest thing to an independent view. School staff tend to find the inspection process very stressful and governors need to consider what they can do to support them during and after the inspection.

Examination and test results

Another comparatively independent source of information about the progress of the school is provided by the examination and test results for SATs. The school should provide the governors with a detailed account of these and an opportunity to discuss them in relation to previous results and the information which is now provided locally and nationally about the results of schools serving similar areas. Many secondary schools test pupils on entry to the school as well as studying their results at Key Stage 2 so that they can make an assessment of likely examination results.

Governing bodies are now required to give predicted targets for their pupils and these will be based on previous results.

Attendance records

If pupils are to learn well, it is important that they attend school regularly. Some schools have a higher record of truancy than others and it is important that governors are aware of the extent to which pupils are away from school without a reason. Some information about this may be part of the headteacher's report but governors may need to ask questions about how much unauthorised absence there is and what the school is doing about it. It may also be useful to enquire about the extent to which parents are asking permission to take children on holiday during term time and what the school does to discourage this.

Linked with this will be information about exclusions. This should be part of the headteacher's report. Governors in schools where exclusions are common should look out for any bias in the population excluded.

Progress of the school development plan and curriculum plans

Schools are required to produce a development plan and to update this annually. The plan should be a joint effort by headteacher, staff and governors and should set out clearly the way in which the planning is to fulfil the aims of the school. The plan should include long-term, medium-term and short-term items with a time scale for each. There should also be an allocation of responsibility for each item and the plan should include costing both in time and money and plans for evaluation. Progress with the plan should be reported to governors regularly.

The overall plan will include plans for developments on all fronts. Some will be curriculum plans and some plans for personal, social and health education and for staff development. There may be plans for developing areas of the school in various ways, perhaps renewing facilities or changing organisation. All the plans should reflect the aims and vision of the school.

The school development plan gives governors a picture of where the school is aiming to go and its progress towards the goals set. It should also offer them an opportunity to be involved in the school's development.

Financial information

Governors should be kept informed about the way in which the school is managing its resources. In many governing bodies this will be the primary responsibility of a finance committee but other committees and the governing body as a whole need to be aware of the financial situation as many of the decisions which governors may take may have financial implications. The annual report to parents must contain a financial statement.

Newsletters to parents

Many schools send regular newsletters to parents and these contain general information about the school which will be of interest to governors.

Information about comparable schools

Benchmarks against which schools can measure their performance are available nationally and locally. The publication of examination results and SATs results provides governors with information against which to compare their schools' performance. Local authorities also publish a good deal of information about schools in their area which serve a similar purpose.

Information deliberately sought by governors

There are a number of ways in which governors can seek out information.

Visits to the school

Governors may visit the school on various occasions. Governors will almost certainly be invited to particular events such as plays, concerts, assemblies and presentation evenings; these give a picture of some of the work of the school. Governors may also visit the school by arrangement to see work going on in classrooms.

Ground rules for visits

A governing body needs to establish ground rules for visits. Arrangements should normally be made through the headteacher. Generally speaking it is not a good idea for governors to make notes about what they are seeing while they are actually in the classroom. This tends to be worrying for teachers, who see note-taking as a process which inspectors undertake. It is good idea to make notes after the event however, especially if the observer will be expected to report back to the rest of the governors.

Observing in primary schools

In arranging to observe classes at work in a primary school governors may spend time in different classes in turn, perhaps starting with the youngest children and moving upwards so that they can see how work develops as children grow older. One of the advantages of observing in a primary school is that it is fairly easy to join in the work going on at some point in the lesson. This is more difficult but not impossible in a secondary school.

Observing in secondary schools

In a secondary school governors may decide to observe lessons in a particular subject or to shadow a particular form or individual pupil through a morning or afternoon. Or governors may observe a series of lessons perhaps starting with the youngest pupils and working their way up through the age groups. This may take several visits but can be very informative.

Observation of teaching

Governors need to spend time observing in classrooms in order to learn about what is actually happening in the school. This is probably the best way to learn about the school. It helps governors to get to know the teachers as well as the headteacher and creates a situation in which they come to know and trust one another. It also gives governors a chance to understand the curriculum as it actually happens in the classroom, gives them insight into the teaching process and helps them to appreciate the role of the teacher. In the long run it will help governors to make informed decisions in which the staff can have confidence. It is important to remember that governors are not observing as an inspector but in an open-minded and non-judgemental way using the opportunity to become more informed about the school.

Some governing bodies have a rota for visits to observe teaching and each governor gives a brief report of what he or she has seen to the whole governing body. Another practice is to have a duty governor rota by which each governor is responsible for a month for any activities which involve governors such as appointment interviews, discussions about exclusion, parents' meetings and so on. This will not be easy for governors who have a full-time job but many schools manage to make this kind of programme work.

Observation is something we do all the time, using not only the sense of sight but also hearing, smell, touch and sometimes taste. We select things out of what we observe, sometimes because we have a particular purpose for observing but also because our previous experience makes us aware that some things are more significant than others. In crossing the road, for example, we are likely to concentrate on traffic rather than pedestrians or the surrounding scenery. Teachers tend to observe more systematically and with greater purpose in the classroom than they would in everyday life. This enables them to make formative assessments about pupils and to modify their next move appropriately.

In observing teaching, we are all conditioned by our own school experience and will be using this as a basis of comparison. All observers bring to the task of observation their own view of what is important and what is good practice even though they may not be professionally involved in education. It is all too easy to see as good those things which accord with one's own view and to ignore the fact that there are as many good ways of teaching as there are good teachers. Teaching is a very personal activity. It is important to know in advance what the teacher is trying to do and to be open to a variety of ways of working.

In observing teaching it is easy to concentrate on the teacher's performance. This is only part of what is happening. It is necessary to look at the relationships and interaction with and among the pupils and at the classroom environment.

There is also the problem that having an observer in the room changes the situation for both teacher and pupils. The way it changes the situation will depend a good deal on the teacher. Some people are more disturbed by being observed than others and some very good teachers may be among this group.

Every classroom yields a range of evidence that can be studied, including the following.

Written material by the teacher

An observer in the classroom is unlikely to have access to the teacher's notes but it is a good idea to ask before the lesson what the material to be studied will be. The teacher may also write on the board and this gives information not only about what is being studied but also about the teacher's views of what the pupils can manage.

Pupils' work

A good deal can be learned by looking at pupils' work. The observer may note such things as presentation, level of content, progress and development over a period, comments and marking by the teacher and the extent to which work is differentiated to match ability. Many classrooms will have pupils' work displayed and this too can be informative. The teacher's approach to homework may also be evident. Has he or she realistic expectations about it? Is enough time given to setting it? Are the pupils clear about what they have to do? Has it been marked conscientiously?

Teacher performance and behaviour

Here the observer can look at such things as whether the teaching methods used seem to be appropriate for the material to be learned and the particular group, the organisation of the lesson and variety of approach, particularly at times of changing activity, expository skills, questioning skills, pupil participation, discussion leadership, use of resources, pace and use of paralinguistic forms of communication both on the part of the teacher and the pupils. Is there evidence of good planning? Is there challenge, progression and rigour in what is offered? Does the teacher stimulate thinking on the part of the pupils? Are there open-ended questions and questions which make pupils really think as well as questions which test recall?

The level of control and discipline will also be evident and the observer may notice the ways in which the teacher deals with difficult behaviour. Does he or she handle this calmly, diffusing the problem and getting the pupils concerned back to work?

The observer can also see whether the teacher has a high level of competence in the subject being taught and has the kind of passionate, enthusiastic approach which is likely to inspire pupils. The teaching style may be different according to the subject as well as according to the individual.

Pupil performance and behaviour

This involves looking at responsiveness, involvement of individuals, work in small groups and work with the whole group, contribution to discussion, body language and so on.

Pupil–teacher interaction

Observation here involves looking at the relationship of teacher and pupils. Is it a caring one? Is the teacher approachable? How does the teacher speak to the pupils? Does the teacher involve all the pupils? Is there any difference in the way boys and girls are treated? How does the teacher react to individual needs? Is there any differentiation in the work given to pupils of differing abilities? It also involves noting the way pupils speak to the teacher, the enthusiasm generated, the extent to which the pupils are prepared to do as the teacher asks.

Pupil–pupil interaction

There may be opportunities for observing how pupils relate to each other in a lesson, depending on the subject studied. If the pupils are working in pairs or groups, how well do they manage? Do they all contribute to the work in hand? To what extent do pupils support and help each other, argue with each other about the material in hand when appropriate and treat each other's contributions to the lesson?

The environment

Where a teacher is able to work in a subject base or his or her own classroom, it becomes possible to observe such things as the organisation and appearance of the room, the extent, appropriateness and function of display and the preparation of the room for the particular lesson. Does the material displayed serve to stimulate the pupils? Is there a variety of pupils' work displayed?

In some lessons, such as physical education, science and technology, issues of health and safety are important. It can also be interesting to look at how pupils are seated. In some lessons teachers will want them to have their own places. In other lessons they sit where they choose and this may have an effect on their behaviour. Teachers also vary in whether they like pupils to sit in groups or in rows. It is interesting to note when a teacher is conducting a whole-class discussion whether there is any pattern in the selection of pupils invited to answer questions. It is possible that pupils at the extreme left and right of the teacher will be noticed less than those in the middle of the room. It is also interesting to note whether more boys than girls are invited to answer or conversely.

The governors of Manor House school decided that they needed to know more about what was actually happening in the classrooms. They agreed that they needed to spend time visiting to find out at first hand how teachers were working. They went on to agree that they would each spend a half-day in the school observing in a classroom first finding out from the teachers concerned what should be happening and then looking to see what went on. They would then spend a Saturday morning discussing what they had seen and with the help of the headteacher and teacher governors would try to set down what they could be looking for.

This all went well. They were agreed that they were looking in order to find out, not as inspectors. They worked in groups of three, first exchanging information on their experiences in the classroom and then setting down the positive things they might look for and then the things they would be concerned to see. The headteacher and teacher governors joined the groups while they were working and added ideas. The groups reported in a plenary session and one member took the lists that the groups had made and put them together to form a guide to classroom observation.

They went on to agree that two governors would arrange to visit each term and would report back to the governors at the next full meeting. Each pair would look at a different age group so that over a period all age groups would be observed.

Governor links with classes or departments

Visits to the school may be conditioned by the arrangements made with the school for governors to have a special link with an individual class in a primary school or a department in a secondary school. This gives governors a chance to get to know a class or department more fully, looking at the aims of its work and how it functions in practice. One secondary school governing body made the following statement about its link governors scheme.

The aims of the liaison are as follows:

- To help foster governors' understanding of the work of the school;
- To help foster teachers' understanding of the work of the governing body.

To achieve these aims, governors might:

- Meet the head of department and members of the department by arrangement;
- Become familiar with the appropriate parts of the National Curriculum;
- Become familiar with the department development plan;
- Become familiar with the ethos of the department;
- Become familiar with the working environment of the department;
- Be aware of the organisation of the work of the department, the responsibilities of its members and the grouping of students;
- Have some idea of the numbers taking GCSE and A level courses in the subject and examination results;
- Discuss what the department is doing for students with special needs or exceptional ability;
- Discuss problems and issues with department staff and act as a sounding board;
- Keep members of the department informed about the work of the governing body;
- If possible spend some time observing in classrooms;
- If possible attend occasional department meetings.

A governor might link with a curriculum coordinator in a primary school and have similar experiences. Alternatively governors might link with a primary school class or year group where a statement about the role might have similar aims and include the following:

- Meet the class teacher or head of year by arrangement;
- Become familiar with the appropriate parts of the National Curriculum;
- Become familiar with the teacher's plans for the class or the year group plans;
- Become familiar with the teacher's or teachers' use of the classroom environment;
- Where a year group is concerned, become familiar with the way in which the teachers work together and the responsibilities of each;
- Become familiar with current results of baseline assessment, Standard Assessment Tasks (SATs) and teacher assessment where these are relevant or any other tests given to the children;
- Discuss what the teacher or teachers are doing for children with special educational needs or exceptional ability;
- Discuss problems and issues and act as a sounding board;
- Keep the teacher(s) informed of the work of the governing body;
- Spend some time observing in classroom(s);

- If possible attend occasional year group meetings;
- Act as a friend and support to the teacher(s) concerned.

One difficulty about this role is that teachers may try to use their link governors to lobby them about particular problems with the head or senior staff. This can be tricky and governors need to be careful not to be seen to be taking sides.

Attendance at school events

Governors will be invited to a variety of school events and these can be very revealing. Plays and concerts will give an idea of how well children can perform and of the amount of work which has gone into this kind of event. Secondary schools will probably have a presentation evening of some kind when certificates and prizes are given. These give an impression of the school and the headteacher's report summarises the achievements of the school during the year. Governors may also want to take the opportunity to attend an occasional assembly.

In all these cases governors can observe the part the pupils play. Is assembly simply an event where the headteacher or senior staff do all the work, with the pupils simply following what they are told to do? Or do the pupils have a real part to play? Similarly with plays and concerts, is there evidence that the pupils have done more than learn parts given them by the teachers? Or does it seem that they have taken a real part in putting on the production? How enthusiastic do the pupils seem about what they are doing?

Inviting staff or pupils to committee meetings to discuss their work

This gives governors a real chance to hear about the work of the school and can provide a focal point for many of the meetings. In a secondary school a curriculum committee might gradually work through the various heads of departments, asking each to talk about the general aims the department has for teaching the subject, the ground they aim to cover at each stage, how they manage assessment, particularly at Key Stage 3, and any other aspect which the head of department thinks might be of interest. Secondary school students, possibly sixth-formers, might also be asked to a meeting to talk about the courses they are taking and how they have found them. What have they enjoyed? What has been difficult? What would they say about the course to a student debating whether to take it next year?

At the primary stage curriculum coordinators might be asked to a meeting to talk about their particular specialisms, describing their aims for the children and how they are helping colleagues to achieve these aims. They might also be asked to describe the processes of teacher assessment they are using. A different pattern might be to ask individual class teachers to talk about the work they are doing with their classes, perhaps describing a particular project or the outcomes of a visit.

An important part of such meetings will be the opportunity it gives governors to find out about the work going on in the school and to question teachers about their work.

Questionnaires to pupils and parents

Pupils are a very important source of information about the school, although individual pupils' views may be biased. Questionnaires to a whole year group may reveal a great deal about how children view the school. Questions such as 'What have you really enjoyed in school in the past year?' or 'What have you disliked or found difficult?' give a useful picture of how different aspects of the school are viewed. In the first year of a secondary school it is useful to ask whether the pupils feel they have repeated work done in the primary school.

Young children may not be able to answer a questionnaire in writing but they may be able to colour in smiley or glum faces according to whether they have enjoyed something or not.

It is also valuable to survey parents' views of the school. One secondary school surveyed new parents' reasons for choosing the school and this provided very useful information about the success of their marketing policy. This was followed up with the same parents at the end of their children's first year in the school with another questionnaire which asked questions about how they had found the school. Was the reporting they received satisfactory? Were there any areas in which they would like more information? Were there any areas in which the school had disappointed them?

One primary school surveyed different groups of parents each year asking parents to grade on a five point scale their opinion of the opportunities parents had been given to find out about the school and their child's progress.

Suggested questionnaires for pupils and for parents are given in the Appendix.

Attendance at parents' evenings

There will be a variety of occasions when governors are able to meet parents and attend their meetings. Some of these may be meetings arranged by the Parent–Teacher Association which will have an agenda of their own. They may give governors an idea of how parents view the school. A different kind of parents' meeting is where the parents are invited to discuss their children's progress with the teachers. This may give governors a chance to chat to parents while they are waiting to see teachers and to get an impression of how they view what is happening to their children at school. A question about the age of the child and an enquiry about how he or she is getting on often gives an insight into the parents' picture of the school and how satisfied they are with what is happening. It may take a bit of courage to go up to strangers and ask them questions but this can be very revealing.

Informal sources of information

In addition to the sources of information listed above there are many opportunities to get an impression of the school from casual observation.

The appearance of the school

This is a very important aspect because new parents will make judgements about the school from its appearance. Is it clean and tidy? What sort of an impression does someone get on walking into the building? Is it clear what a visitor should do? Is there a display of children's work about the building as well as in the class-rooms? What about the grounds? Is there litter about? Are the grounds well kept?

Reception of visitors

The way a visitor is received or the phone is answered makes an immediate impres-sion. This may pose problems in a very small school where there is only part-time secretarial help and the headteacher may find he or she has to interrupt teaching to receive visitors. In a larger school where there is full-time help the school secretary will have an important role in making visitors feel welcome. New governors will be in a position to judge this when first becoming a governor and going into the school unknown to the staff.

Staff–pupil relationships

A very important aspect of the school is the relationships between the staff and the pupils. Do teachers and other staff appear to be friendly to pupils or do they give the impression of being always out to catch someone doing the wrong thing? Are they encouraging to children? How do they deal with those who misbehave? How do they talk to pupils?

Behaviour of pupils about the school

As governors go about the school they will get an impression of the way that the pupils behave. Do they go around behaving in a reasonable manner, not pushing and shoving each other? Do they give way to adults? In particular governors may note how they behave at the beginning and end of school and at lunchtime. What sort of an impression do they make coming out of school?

The appearance of pupils

While the appearance of pupils, particularly at the primary stage, may be as much a reflection on their parents as on the school, schools do have an influence on and usually have rules about how pupils appear. A school may or may not have a uniform; whatever it is the pupils will do their best to make it accord with the current fashion, which may be at variance with what the staff of the school would like. An observer can note whether pupils are reasonably tidy and how far they are conforming to any uniform.

Governors' relationships with teaching and support staff

Governors will get an impression of the school from their relationships with the staff, both the teaching staff and the support staff. People who are happy and relaxed in their work will be ready to talk about it frankly and give an idea of how the school looks from their point of view.

Involvement with the PTA

Parent governors in particular need to involve themselves in PTA activities because these give an opportunity to talk to parents about how they are finding the school.

Comments from members of the community

Governors are likely to be on the receiving end of comments about the school from parents and other members of the local community. Some of these may be positive comments. Others may be complaints. These can be tricky, since governors need, on the one hand, to be ambassadors for the school, making positive statements about it when they get the chance and on the other hand they may be the recipient of some fairly negative comments. Where governors receive complaints it is a good idea to check whether the person complaining has said anything to the head or staff of the school and then, depending on the nature of the complaint, decide what to do about it. The governors should have a complaints procedure and the person complaining may be referred to this. He or she should be encouraged to use it but the person concerned may be unwilling to go through official channels and expect an individual governor to do something about the problem. It may be a good idea to ask other governors whether they have had any similar complaints and what they have done about them. The information can be fed back to the headteacher in tactful way and discuss what can be done about the complaint. *School Governors: A Guide to the Law* states that:

> No governor should deal with complaints alone. You should make sure that the person making the complaint and the person being complained about are allowed to state their case and be treated fairly. You should put the decisions and the reasons for them in writing. You should tell the person making the complaint about their right to appeal if the decision is given against them.
>
> (DfEE 1997: 17)

This should be part of the complaints procedure.

Questions to consider

1   What has happened following the action plan made after our last inspection?
2   How do this year's test/examination results compare with those of previous years?

2   Is our attendance record satisfactory? If not, is there anything more we should be doing to improve it? Are too many parents taking their children on holiday during term time?

4   Would it be a good idea to arrange regular visits by governors to observe work in classrooms?

5   Would it be a good idea for individual governors to link with departments or classes?

6   Should we invite members of staff or pupils to meet us to talk about their work?

7   What could we find out from the pupils and the parents? Could we use parents' evenings to ask questions about parents' views of the school?

8   What impression does the school make when you first walk into it? Is the appearance attractive? How do the pupils behave about the school? What sort of welcome does the visitor get? What sort of reception does one get when telephoning the school? What impression do the pupils make when coming out of school?

Chapter 6

Policy making

The governing body of a school is responsible for its policies. The actual wording of the policies may be done by groups of governors or by the head and staff or by a combination of these people, but it is the task of the governors to see that the school has policies in all the areas required by law and in other areas in which it is desirable to have guidance for action. Governors also need to see that all who work in the school are aware of the policies which affect them and carry out the intentions of the policies in action.

A framework for policy writing

A policy is a statement of intent, giving the principles that guide action and instructions for action. It is helpful to have a framework for policy writing so that all policies conform to a pattern and can be seen to be a way of fulfilling the schools' aims and objectives. Policies will vary according to the area in question but most are likely to contain statements such as the following.

Overall philosophy and principles operating in the area in question

Where it seems to make sense there could be a reference to the overall aims and vision of the school, for example an equal opportunities policy might start with a statement such as the following:

> The governors, headteacher and staff of this school believe that all pupils should have equal opportunities to make use of what the school has to offer, whether they are boys or girls, members of ethnic minorities or indigenous population, middle or working class, fast or slow learners.

The attitudes expected

The policy needs a statement about the view of the topic the school wishes to take, for example a curriculum policy might include the following statement:

> Teachers should have high expectations for all pupils whatever their ability.

The people to whom the policy applies

This will nearly always be the teachers but sometimes the pupils and support staff, for example a health and safety policy might include a statement such as the following:

> All members of the staff of the school, including both teachers and support staff, must be concerned with health and safety and with preventing personal injury, health hazards and damage to property. Pupils also need to be taught safe ways of working in such subjects as science and physical education and to be encouraged to be generally aware of health and safety issues.

The people who are responsible for seeing that the policy is implemented

As an example, a special needs policy might make a statement about the distribution of responsibility between the SEN coordinator and the other teachers such as the following:

> The SEN coordinator is responsible for maintaining the school's register of children with special educational needs, for working with colleagues to ensure that provision is made for these pupils, for drawing up individual education plans for them when appropriate, for advising colleagues on how to work with these pupils and when appropriate for providing extra teaching for them. All teachers are responsible for the learning and progress of pupils with special educational needs in their classes.

Specific arrangements needed

A curriculum policy will need to make reference to the literacy and numeracy programmes in the primary school. A secondary school may need statements about opportunities to take a second modern language or three separate sciences.

The organisation of any material resources or equipment

A primary school may organise resources such as mathematical or scientific equipment as a whole school or year group and will need statements about how this may be borrowed and used. A secondary school may need to make a statement about the use of information technology, particularly if computers are not available in quantity in every department.

Arrangements for monitoring the implementation of the policy

It will be normal practice to review progress where areas of the curriculum or special needs are concerned, but there is also a need to make it part of a policy in areas such as behaviour where regular reviewing of what has happened and how successfully it has been dealt with is less common but necessary. The policy should make it clear whose task it is to review implementation.

The support available to teachers

In the case of a behaviour policy, the rewards and sanctions available need to be stated and teachers need to know to whom they can refer cases which they feel need more serious treatment.

Relevant staff development

In many areas of school life there will be a need for training of staff. Many policies need to state the opportunities which will be available to staff and in some cases state whether it is essential that they take the opportunity for training.

The place of any links with contributory or transfer schools and colleges

There needs to be a statement in most areas of curriculum about the nature of such links and what is expected from them.

Palethorpe high school needed to make a policy for curriculum. They had one which had been drawn up some years ago but felt that it was now out of date and needed to be rewritten. The task of doing this was given to the curriculum committee, which included both the headteacher and one of the teacher governors.

They decided to split into pairs and set down anything they could think of which ought to be included. They then came together to discuss what they had concluded. One pair had stressed the importance of helping students to become independent learners able to use information technology to help their learning. The need for creativity in all subjects was also listed. Another pair had listed the need to provide for those students who wished to take three separate sciences and two foreign languages and for work experience to be available for all students. The importance of continuity from the primary school and from year to year was stressed and the need to see that there was a full programme of personal and social education which included sex education and dealt with relationships. Equal opportunities for all students was listed and the need to see that students with special needs or exceptional ability were catered for. There was also concern that students were developing positive attitudes to other people whatever their race or creed or gender.

When all the information had been collected one person took the lists away and used the information to write the policy using the policy brief which the school had adopted. This was then discussed first by the curriculum committee, then by the staff and then agreed by the full governing body.

Names and dates

The names of those who were involved in compiling the policy should be given, also the date when it was agreed by the governing body and subsequently the dates when it was reviewed.

Legally required policies

Some policies or statements are legally required and others are recommended but not statutory. Governors need to be sure that all the legally required statements are included. They are as follows:

Action plan following inspection

The governing body must draw up an action plan following an inspection within forty days of receiving the report. This will normally take account of the findings of the inspection and state what will be done about them, allocating responsibility and a time scale for each action. Copies of the action plan have to be sent to Ofsted and the LEA and those who appoint the foundation governors and/or the diocese in the case of church schools.

Annual governors' report to parents

This must state how the governing body has put into practice its plans for the school since the last report. It must be given to parents at least two weeks before the annual parents' meeting. More details about the content of this report are given in Chapter 11.

Charging policy

A governing body must have a policy on charging for any activities which are outside the normal curriculum of the school and take place outside school hours. Examples might be individual or group music tuition, school visits if these are residential or if they involve travel outside school hours. Trips which take place during school hours must be free although the school may invite voluntary contributions from parents. Charges may not exceed the actual cost of the activity although an allowance may be made for the costs of teachers to supervise, but only if those teachers have been given a separate contract to provide the optional extra.

A residential activity which takes place largely during school time or which meets examination or National Curriculum requirements must be free but a charge may be made for board and lodging.

Curriculum

The LEA has to publish a statement setting out its policy for curriculum for schools in its area. Governors must take account of this when producing their own policy statement. They must take account of any views expressed by the local community and the chief of police and make sure that their policy fits in with the National Curriculum. Any changes must be included in the annual report to parents. The policy might include general aims, statements about what is to be taught at each level, how the most and least able are to be dealt with, teaching methods and approaches and arrangements for ensuring continuity.

Health and safety policy

Voluntary and foundation schools must, by law, have a policy on health and safety. LEA schools will have a statement from the local authority but governors need to discuss this and may wish to write their own version to meet the particular needs of their school.

The governing body should make regular assessments of any risk factors and see that there are procedures for carrying out the LEA's policy, or, in the case of foundation and voluntary schools, procedures for carrying out their own policy. Governors should also monitor health and safety.

The policy statement should include information about the overall organisation for ensuring health and safety and the roles of those concerned with seeing that there is good practice. It should also include reference to arrangements for first aid.

Pupils' behaviour policy

The 1996 Education Act makes the headteacher responsible for taking measures to ensure good behaviour in line with any written statement of general principles prepared by the governors for putting these general principles into practice and for dealing with individual cases of misbehaviour. The 1997 Education Act gave additional powers to schools to deal with misbehaviour and made it compulsory for all schools to publish a discipline policy. Schools may keep pupils in after school without the permission of their parents and may exclude pupils for up to fifteen days in any one term.

The policy should set out what is expected by way of behaviour from pupils, give ways in which good behaviour can be rewarded and state the sanctions available for misbehaviour. There should be reference to bullying and how it is to be dealt with unless the school also has an anti-bullying policy.

It is important that both pupils and parents should be fully aware of the behaviour policy and of their part in implementing it.

Staff discipline and grievance procedures

Governors are responsible with the headteacher for staff discipline and should also have grievance procedures set out so that staff are aware of what to do if they have a grievance or complaint about their employment. The headteacher and the governors have the power to suspend any member of staff on full pay if this should prove necessary.

Special educational needs policy

The *Education (Special Educational Needs) Regulations* (DfEE 1994a) quoted in the *Governors' Handbook* by the Advisory Centre for Education (ACE 1998: 45–6) requires all schools to publish their policy. This must contain the following information.

Basic information about the school's special educational provision

- the objectives of the policy
- the name of the school's special educational needs coordinator (SENCO) or teacher responsible for the day-to-day operation of the special educational needs policy
- the arrangements for coordinating educational provision for pupils with special educational needs
- any special educational needs specialism and any special units
- any building adaptations and special features.

Information about the school's policies for identification, assessment and provision for all pupils with special educational needs

- the allocation of resources to and among pupils
- the identification, assessment, monitoring and review procedures
- arrangements for providing access to the curriculum for pupils with special educational needs
- how children with special educational needs are integrated into the school as a whole
- criteria for evaluating the success of the special educational needs policy
- any arrangements for considering complaints about special educational needs provision within the school.

Information about the school's staffing policies and partnership with bodies beyond the school

- the school's arrangements for special educational needs in-service training
- use made of teachers and facilities from outside the school including support services
- arrangements for partnership with parents
- links with other mainstream and special schools, including arrangements when pupils change or leave school
- links with health and social services, educational welfare services and any voluntary organisations.

The school prospectus must include a summary of the SEN policy and the governing body must report on the implementation and effectiveness of the policy in its annual report to parents.

Governors may also like to consider whether their policy for pupils with special educational needs should in addition cover the needs of those pupils who have exceptional ability. Alternatively they may like to make this a separate policy. This is not a legal requirement.

Sex education policy

Governors of primary schools may decide whether or not the school should provide sex education in addition to that which is part of the National Curriculum and if so what should be included. They should keep a written record of their decision. If they decide to include sex education in the curriculum they should have a policy which sets out what should be included and the general principles which staff should have in mind in teaching it. Secondary schools must provide sex education and governors need to consider what should be included, by whom it should be taught and in what context.

Other desirable policies

Equal opportunities

It is against the law to discriminate on grounds of sex, race or disability and schools must be sure that they provide equal opportunities for all pupils. The policy needs to deal with admissions to the school, ensuring that pupils are admitted regardless of gender, race, social or ethnic background. The curriculum should be equally available to all pupils and teaching methods and materials reflect this. Schemes of work and syllabuses should provide for all abilities. Issues related to equality and discrimination should be discussed and pupils encouraged to support the equal opportunities policy.

The policy of equal opportunities must also apply to the staff and particularly to appointments.

Assessment and recording

Schools, particularly secondary schools where pupils meet a variety of teachers and approaches, need to have a common method of assessing pupils' learning and recording progress. The aim of assessment is to help pupils to become effective learners by giving them feedback on their performance and suggesting ways forward. Marking of work should be similarly carried out by all teachers and should as far as possible be positive. If grades or marks are used they should be used consistently by all staff and their meaning should be clear to pupils and their parents. There should be clear criteria for each mark or grade and these should be known to pupils.

Records of pupils' progress should be common throughout the school and should be updated at regular intervals.

Schools are legally required to report to parents on each pupil's progress and there needs to be agreement on the form of this report and the way that reports are completed.

Additional policies

Schools may also wish to have policies for anti-bullying, assemblies, careers' education, child protection, drugs education, the education of able pupils, health education, homework, induction of new teachers, lettings, pupils' uniform, staff development, in-service education and pay.

Questions to consider

1   Do we have a framework for policy writing?
2   Are there policies in all the areas in which they are legally required?
3   Are there other areas in which we should have policies?
4   Do we have a regular programme of reviewing policies?

Chapter 7

Finance and premises

Sources of finance

The finance for schools comes from four sources – government grants to the local authority, non-domestic rates, the council tax and income from fees and other direct charges. The largest source is the grant from central government. This is arrived at by assessing how much each authority will need to spend to provide a standard level of service and is known as the Standard Spending Assessment (SSA). The grant is known as the Revenue Support Grant (RSG) and is financed mainly from taxes. It is not a grant specifically for education but is intended to cover all the services provided by the local authority. The way it is spent is a matter for locally elected councillors, advised by their officers.

During the 1990s local authorities had to delegate a large share of their education spending directly to the schools under a scheme known as local management of schools (LMS). LEAs have had to submit to central government and publish the schemes they are using to decide on the amount to be delegated to each school. At least 80 per cent of the money should be given on the basis of numbers of pupils in the school. This has made it important for schools to attract pupils since the finance they will be given to run the school will depend to a large extent on numbers. There will also be additional allowances for small schools and pupils with special educational needs.

A new system started in April 1999 in which the government asked LEAs to delegate a larger share of the funds available to schools under a scheme known as Fair Funding. LEAs may retain money for the following:

- strategic management (chief education officer and staff, corporate planning, audit and statutory duties)
- access (school places, transport and admissions)
- school improvement (as set out in the development plan which the LEA has to submit to the Department of Education and Employment)
- special educational needs including making statements for children who need them.

In the past LEAs have been able to keep back money for building and maintenance, minor capital works, school meals, central support services such as personnel and payroll, catering and cleaning, curriculum, advisory and training services and school library services. Money for these items of expenditure will now be delegated to schools but it will be possible for schools to buy back these services. Finance committees will need to make decisions about whether to buy services from the LEA or to buy them elsewhere.

Cost management

The way that governors and the headteacher and senior staff manage finance is important for the success of the school. Knight (1993) differentiates between money management which is the way you spend your money and cost management:

> Cost management is not just identifying costs and reducing them, valuable though this is, but also costing time utilisation, the educational process and its outputs, and alternative educational strategies. You will only be a really effective financial manager if you can both plan and balance your budget – the money side – and cost your operation, its outcomes and alternatives.
>
> (Knight 1993: 6)

Knight points out that a 10 per cent increase in financial resources does not necessarily lead to a 10 per cent increase in learning. In short, governor need to look at the effect of the school's finances on its performance.

Until 1999 governors have been responsible for the school's spending on the following:

- teaching staff
- support staff
- rent and local taxes
- internal building maintenance
- equipment, including furniture and fittings as well as educational equipment
- fuel and lighting
- books and stationery
- office needs, such as postage, telephone, reprographics and printing
- school visits and staff travel
- examination fees
- cleaning materials and equipment.

The extent to which there will be additional areas of financial commitment will depend on the extent to which the schools in an area decide to buy back services from the local authority. Some may prefer to buy such services from an independent provider.

Setting priorities

In setting out priorities for spending governors will need to identify those costs which are fixed. These will include staffing, heating, lighting and basic building and equipment maintenance. It is also important to budget for both maintenance and development. Most of the budget will be maintenance and some development will incur future maintenance costs. Some equipment and furniture will have a limited life and budgets need to include provision over time for replacement and there should be an inventory kept of such items. Budgets also need to be related to pupil outcomes. Is it possible to see whether increased spending in a particular area has led to increased learning? How will governors know whether agreed goals have been achieved?

Priorities will be set as part of the school development plan, which should include costing for each item.

Governors should be aware of the way in which money is allocated to budget holders within the school. Money can be allocated on the basis of the previous year's spending, on requests for money for development and maintenance or as a grant with or without strings or recommendations. It is possible to link grants to expected advances in performance and also to build in incentives to save. For example, if a department or class spends less on photocopying, it may keep the savings. It is a good idea every few years to undertake what is known as zero budgeting, in which the school starts with a clean slate and examines the requirements of each class or department. This is too difficult to do every year but there should be a limit to the extent that the budget is allocated on a historic basis.

One item which should be a feature of all planned expenditure is insurance. There will be some LEA cover and governors should be aware of this but there may also be a need for the school to have its own insurance.

Control and monitoring

Governors need to see that proper systems are set up for controlling spending. Funds must be spent as authorised and there must be systems for authorising spending and recording what has been spent. Monitoring compares the amount actually spent against what was estimated and this needs to be done regularly. Budget holders need regular updates about the state of the funds for which they are responsible giving the total budget, the items bought, the expected expenditure to date, the actual expenditure to date and the variance between the two. As far as possible different people should be responsible for the separate functions of budgeting. For example, different people should be responsible for the cash receipts, for banking, ordering, authorising expenditure, signing cheques and keeping accounts and records.

Value for money

Inspections of schools are asked to consider whether the school is giving value for money and this needs to be in the mind of all those who are making decisions about the budget. Schools are now given information about comparable schools which lists costs as well as achievement. Governors need to compare their school with others to see if they are offering good value for money.

Within the school, areas of the budget need to be delegated and the governors should be aware of how this is done. In a secondary school, heads of department may have delegated funding. In a primary school, each teacher or each curriculum coordinator may have a budget allocation. It is a good idea for each budget holder to be asked to make a plan for spending at the beginning of each financial year under headings such as stationery, books, photocopying and so on. This need not be a plan to which they are tightly tied, but planning will make people aware of the need to consider how the spending is going. It is also important to be clear about who will authorise spending.

There should be a school culture in which all those who control spending are aware of the need to spend carefully. This is helped when there are regular updates on spending patterns. There should also be opportunity to carry money forward from one year to the next so that there is not a rush to spend up at the end of the year.

Local authorities have to ensure that there is competitive tendering for cleaning, grounds maintenance, school catering and vehicle maintenance. Governors can choose whether to join in LEA schemes or make their own arrangements. Where governors choose to make their own arrangements it is important to get competitive tenders. It is also important to use any opportunities offered to get discounts by prompt payment.

Raising money

The 1986 Education Act provides that governors have control of the school premises outside of school hours subject to any general direction by the local authority and can set charges and receive any income derived from lettings provided that any expenses are defrayed, although there may be standard charges for statutory lettings such as council meetings or elections.

The school may also consider various ways of raising funds for its own purposes. The following methods might be used:

- eliciting donations, including covenanting
- sponsorship of individual effort
- mufti days
- sales of donated items, car boot sales, jumble sales
- fund-raising events which provide enjoyment, such as socials, dances, wine-tasting
- sales of tickets to school events such as plays or concerts
- games of chance such as lotteries and raffles
- sponsorship of an event or feature of the school by an outside firm or person, which can be a form of advertising for the firm concerned.

A study of the impact of local management of schools by Maychell (1994) found that 73 per cent of primary schools and 78 per cent of secondary schools had money from their Parent–Teacher Association; 61 per cent of primary schools and 40 per cent of secondary schools generated income from fund-raising activities; 54 per cent of primary schools and 47 per cent of secondary schools had income from lettings and 35 per cent of primary schools and 48 per cent of secondary schools had money from sponsors.

The study also found that since the advent of LMS there was a large increase in the amount of time that headteachers spent on administration.

School funds need to be properly managed with clear guidelines for spending and recording and should be audited regularly.

Evaluating the budget

Knight (1993) suggests that there are three aspects to evaluating the budget:

1   Financial efficiency – comparing the out-turn budget with the start-of-year estimates.
2   Resource efficiency – looking at what the money was spent on.
3   Effectiveness – assessing whether the expenditure achieved the outcomes hoped for.

(Knight 1993: 151)

Evaluation of the last of these items is the one most likely to be forgotten in the general pressures on staff and governors but it is important to set time aside to consider how effective the spending has been.

Equal opportunities

In considering how money should be spent by a school, governors need to consider whether everyone is getting an equal opportunity to benefit from the way money is being spent. Is there any group of pupils or any individuals who are getting a smaller or larger share of the money available? Can this be justified? Do certain groups of pupils see more of the most experienced teachers or spend time in smaller classes or occupy the best accommodation? Do pupils with special needs including the most able and gifted children get a fair share of the resources available? Do some subjects get a better deal than others? All these allocations of resources may be justifiable and it may be desirable to discriminate positively for some children but it is a good idea to examine spending from time to time with equality of opportunity in mind.

Staff audit

Governors need to be aware of the overall patterns of teachers' pay as they will affect budgeting in the future. Governors need to know the costs of full-time and part-time staff, the age and experience of existing staff and the distribution of allowances. This will enable them to be aware of probable rises in costs or of opportunities for reducing staff costs by, for example, appointing a newly qualified teacher when an experienced teacher leaves.

The most recent government plans for teachers' pay will require consideration of whether some teachers should be paid more than others for their skills in the classroom. This will need assessment of competence and skills both by the headteacher and also by an outside assessor. Knight (1993) suggests the following criteria for differentiating teachers' salaries:

- qualifications and training (initial and in-service)
- quantity of work, i.e. hours worked
- role and responsibilities
- level and demands of work, i.e. differences of subjects or students
- quality of work, i.e skills and competences demonstrated
- performance, i.e. achievement of defined targets against pre-set criteria.

Knight (1993: 163)

Governors are also responsible for deciding the pay of headteachers and deputy headteacher(s). This requires an agreement on targets for heads and deputies and an assessment of whether they have achieved them.

Cost of in-service training

The budget needs to cover not only the cost of teachers attending courses but also the cost of supply cover for those courses which take place during the day. Governors need to be concerned with the use the school makes of in-service education of teachers (INSET). It should be something planned by the head-teacher in consultation with individual members of staff, so that the needs of the school are met as well as the needs of individuals. There is some evidence from research that in-service training is less effective in its results when teachers are allowed to go to whatever courses they choose without any overall planning (Mortimore et al. 1988). All teachers need to be involved in INSET from time to time.

Premises

Governing bodies need to be clear about their responsibilities with regard to the school premises and those of the LEA. The local authority is the owner of the school premises in the case of LEA schools and therefore has responsibility for their upkeep and condition in the long term but some of this responsibility is passed to governors. Governors' responsibility may vary somewhat from one area to another and from one type of school to another though recent legislation has increased governors' responsibilities in all areas.

Governors need to see that the school is kept in good repair and that it is kept clean. Schools may choose to buy in to an LEA scheme for cleaning or may prefer to make its own arrangements locally. If more than three people are employed in cleaning, the school must get competitive tenders. It is a good idea for governors involved in the care of premises to tour the school regularly to see how well it is kept and its state of repair. Governors should check on toilets, ask questions about fire hazards, check whether the playground is more than a bare area, look at the state of repair and decoration in classrooms about the school, see whether it is clear where visitors should go and what sort of impression the school would make to someone entering it for the first time.

Health and safety

An important area for governors to consider is health and safety, including the Health and Safety at Work Act 1974 and the policy and any guidelines issued by the LEA. The school should have a health and safety policy and governors need to take steps to ensure that the buildings and equipment are safe and do not put anyone at risk. The health and safety policy should include:

1   A general statement of policy concerning heath and safety.
2   The organisation which will implement the policy and the functions which have been allocated to individuals.
3   The arrangements for carrying out the policy and for monitoring its effectiveness.

Governors need to be sure that job descriptions include any appropriate statements about the individual's functions in relation to health and safety. Science and physical education departments in particular need to have their own policies and programme for ensuring that pupils work safely. It is a good idea to share the content of these policies with parents so that they can be reassured of their children's safety.

The school needs to have a member of staff with responsibility for health and safety; many schools also have a health and safety committee of staff to watch out for any health and safety hazards and inspect the school for hazards on a regular basis. Governors need to be clear about the arrangements the school makes for first aid and for reporting accidents. The school also needs to have considered how it will respond to emergencies such as fire, floods, explosions and so on.

Governors are responsible for seeing that the school site is kept free from litter, but this is largely a task for the headteacher and staff.

Security has become a particular concern in recent years and governors need to ensure that everything possible has been done to make the school premises secure. This is not easy since many school sites are open and anyone can wander in. Governors have to report on security to parents at the annual meeting each year.

Insurance

Governors need to ensure that the school is covered by insurance either through an LEA scheme or individually. The *School Governor's Manual* (Croner 1999: 2–7) suggests that insurance should cover:

- the risks incurred by the governing body, including governor indemnification
- negligence towards employees and third party
- theft, fire, building contents, vehicles
- risks incurred by fund-raising events
- any activity that occurs in relation to the school premises that falls outside the normal educational activity or business of the school.

Questions to consider

1   Do we consider whether the way we spend the money available has an effect on pupils' learning and development?
2   Do we differentiate between development and maintenance costs?
3   Do we have a programme for replacement of items of equipment as they wear out? Is there an inventory of such items?
4   Do we know how spending is delegated within the school?
5   Is each year's budget decided only on the pattern of past spending or is there scope for new developments?
6   Are we getting value for money? How do we know this?
7   Are we using all the possible avenues for fund-raising?
8   How do we evaluate the way we are spending money?
9   How do we make decisions about the pay of staff, especially the head-teacher and deputy head(s)?
10   Are we spending enough on in-service training?
11   Are we satisfied with the state of repair of our premises?
12   Are we satisfied with the cleaning of our school?
13   Are we happy with the arrangements for health and safety?
14   Are we satisfied with the security arrangements at the school?

Chapter 8

Curriculum and assessment

Teaching and learning

Teaching and learning are the fundamental purposes of a school and governors need to concern themselves with the effectiveness of these activities. The National Curriculum lays down the subjects which should be taught but it is up to the individual teacher to decide how they are taught. There is now a great deal of research into effective teaching and learning and knowledge of what helps pupils to learn.

Teaching and learning are not the same thing. A teacher can appear to teach something but the pupils will not necessarily learn what is being taught unless they are motivated to do so. The teacher has always to consider what will interest and motivate, since pupils must learn for themselves and this involves a personal decision to make the effort to learn. Pupils are generally interested by work which involves them actively and at all stages, but first-hand experience is needed, especially at the primary stage. A teacher can talk about something, but unless the pupils can match the teacher's words from their own experience, understanding will be limited, whereas when they are involved in doing something, handling something or seeing something, they are more likely to understand. The experience of young children is very limited so that primary school teachers need to be aware that what they say may be misunderstood or not understood at all. At the secondary stage it is still important for pupils to see, do and handle but the more able pupils in particular will be much more adept at learning from the words of the teacher.

At the infant and nursery stage of education, much learning will be through play. Teachers will set up play situations which will lead to learning. For example, an infant classroom may have a shop where children play at buying things and learn about money and possibly weights and measures in the process. Children playing in a water tray may be involved finding out about volume and capacity when the teacher suggests finding out how many cups can be filled from one bottle. Much play leads to language development and to the skills of getting along with other people. Play motivates the children and the teacher uses opportunities as they arise to encourage the learning he or she has in mind.

At the junior stage children consolidate the work they have done earlier and move on to a more differentiated programme with literacy and mathematics playing a major part. Approximately an hour a day should be spent on each of these subjects.

In 1999 a review of teaching standards at the secondary school level derived from Ofsted inspections looked at the progress which had been made over recent years and found that good teachers enabled pupils to achieve high standards by:

- building on pupils' earlier attainments
- building on pupils' experience of the world
- setting targets which challenge pupils' own expectations of themselves
- devising strategies for developing pupils' skills
- being aware of gender issues and monitoring work patterns of both sexes.

(Ofsted 1999)

The study found that overall teaching and progress had improved in most subjects. The main exception was information technology, which was reported as being of too low a standard in half the schools and was the least well taught of any subject. Religious education also had a generally lower standard than other subjects, except in GCSE courses, where the work compared favourably. Several subject reports noted that teachers tended to have too low an expectation of pupils, particularly the most and least able. This was true in design and technology, mathematics and geography and the most and least able tended to under-perform in history in a small number of schools.

The National Curriculum

All schools must follow the National Curriculum, which consists of three core subjects – English, mathematics and science – and the foundation subjects of art, citizenship (secondary schools), design and technology, history, geography, information technology, modern foreign languages (secondary schools), music and physical education.

English

The National Curriculum in England: English (DfEE and Qualifications and Curriculum Authority (QCA) 1999a) makes the following statement about the importance of English in pupils' education:

English is a vital way of communicating in school, in public life and internationally. Literature in English is rich and influential, reflecting the experience of people from many countries and times.

In studying English pupils develop skills in speaking, listening, reading and writing. It enables them to express themselves creatively and imaginatively and to communicate with others effectively.

Pupils learn to become enthusiastic and critical readers of stories, poetry and drama as well as non-fiction and media texts.

> The study of English helps pupils understand how language works by looking at its patterns, structures and origins. Using this knowledge pupils can choose and adapt what they say and write in different situations.
>
> (DfEE and QCA 1999a: 1)

At the early stages of education, English teaching is concerned with reading and writing as well as encouraging children to speak confidently and listen to what others have to say. Pupils are introduced to phonics and made aware of sounds as well as learning to recognise whole words and make sense of what is read by using the context. They learn to use full stops and capital letters and question marks.

They go on to learn the rules and conventions of written English and practise planning, drafting and editing their work, learning to speak and write appropriately for different audiences and readerships and take part in discussions. They learn standard English. They develop the ability to take meaning from texts, both fiction and non-fiction, and are able to use inference and deduction. They learn to use punctuation correctly and are taught word classes and grammatical functions.

At the later stages of education, pupils develop their ability to evaluate the use of language, become articulate and fluent speakers for a range of purposes and audiences, contributing effectively to group discussions and using standard English fluently and accurately. They should read and evaluate many kinds of texts and recognise the characteristics of high quality writing, be able to select, compare and synthesise information from different texts and be aware of the ways in which the nature and purpose of media products influence content and meaning. They should write appropriately for a variety of purposes, planning, drafting and redrafting on paper and on screen. They should be taught the principles of grammar and apply them in their writing.

Drama should be part of the English curriculum at all stages.

Governors are responsible for agreeing a literacy policy which

- makes it clear that everyone in the school community can contribute to improving literacy
- includes targets for improvement in literacy standards
- promotes consistency in marking work, checking presentation, spelling and handwriting
- includes a development plan to stimulate interest and enthusiasm for reading
- provides strategies for working with pupils who have reading difficulties
- uses information and communication technology (ICT) to support literacy across the curriculum.

Governors of primary schools are expected to appoint a governor to take particular responsibility for literacy.

All teachers, whatever their subject, need to teach literacy and develop the pupils' ability to express themselves in speech. Language is important for many reasons, not least because much of our thinking is in words and language skills govern the ability to think to some extent. Schools should have a language policy with which everyone is familiar. This will cover some of the same ground as the English policy but will give practice in all subjects in using the skills which English teaching is designed to implant. In every subject there should be opportunities for discussion and for the expression of ideas and views in speech and writing and for adapting these for particular audiences. Almost all subjects include the need to read and even the youngest children need practice in recognising printed and written words relating to their work and play. Secondary schools, in particular, need to look carefully at the difficulty of texts in subjects other than English and consider the help pupils may need in accessing them. Schools also need to have common practice in how the language aspect of work is corrected and assessed.

The literacy hour

From September 1998, primary school teachers have been asked to teach the literacy hour, which is based on the National Literacy Strategy (NLS) (DfEE 1998a). This involves a mixture of whole class and independent work and should include work on words, sentences and texts. A teacher might spend fifteen minutes working with the whole class on a text, perhaps involving both reading and writing. This might be followed by work on words and sentences, with an emphasis on phonics and spelling at the early stages and spelling, grammar and punctuation at the later stages. After this the teacher will provide independent work for the group as a whole, but might teach one group within the class, a different group each day. The work might include guided reading where a group study a text together or guided writing where work might flow from the whole class sessions. A final ten minutes is spent summing up, emphasising teaching points and help the pupils to reflect upon what they have learned.

Effective teachers of literacy

Medwell *et al.* (1998) surveyed the work of 228 teachers identified as effective teachers of literacy and concluded that they had the following characteristics:

- They believed that the purpose of teaching literacy was to enable their pupils to create meaning from text.
- They centred much of their teaching around 'shared' texts which the teacher or children read or wrote together.
- They had strong and coherent personal philosophies about the teaching of literacy which guided their work.
- They had well developed systems for monitoring children's progress and used this information to plan future teaching.
- They had extensive knowledge about literacy.

Mathematics

The *National Curriculum in England: Mathematics* (DfEE and QCA 1999b) makes the following statement about the importance of mathematics in the education of pupils:

Mathematics equips pupils with a uniquely powerful set of tools to understand and change the world. These tools include logical reasoning, problem-solving skills, and the ability to think in abstract ways. Mathematics is important in everyday life, many forms of employment, science and technology, medicine, the economy, the environment and development, and in public decision-making. Different cultures have contributed to the development and application of mathematics. Today, the subject transcends cultural boundaries and its importance is universally recognised. Mathematics is a creative discipline. It can stimulate moments of pleasure and wonder when a pupil solves a problem for the first time, discovers a more elegant solution to that problem, or suddenly sees hidden connections.

(DfEE and QCA 1999b: 1)

In the beginning pupils learn to count, read, write and order numbers to 100 and beyond and start to develop mental calculation skills. They learn about shape and space through practical activity and start to use mathematical language correctly and start to understand place value. They are introduced to the four rules of number and create and describe number patterns. They learn addition and subtraction facts to ten and the two times and ten times tables. They learn to select appropriate materials and equipment to solve problems involving measurement, shape and space.

They go on to develop skills in problem solving and describe number patterns. They begin to understand fractions and their relation to decimals, percentages and their uses. They recall number facts to twenty and multiplication facts to ten times ten and corresponding division facts. They learn to use short and long multiplication and division and use calculators for calculations involving several digits. They select and use appropriate calculation skills to solve geometrical problems and understand properties of shape, position and movement. They learn to select suitable measurement units for length, mass and capacity. They interpret tables, lists and charts used in everyday life and represent and interpret discrete data using graphs and diagrams, bar charts and line graphs.

At the secondary school stage pupils encounter algebraic and geometric proofs and are introduced to a quantitative approach to probability. They learn to select efficient techniques for numerical calculation and algebraic manipulation and to understand and use negative numbers. They learn to use the terms square, positive and negative square root, cube, cube root; use index notation and index laws; use ratio notation and interpret percentages and convert fractions to percentages. They develop a range of strategies for mental calculation and use calculators efficiently and effectively. They generate and plot graphs of simple quadratic and cubic functions; solve geometrical problems; know properties of different shapes and interpret scales on a variety of measuring instruments.

They learn to make appropriate connections between number, algebra, space, shape and measures and handling data, using a range of strategies to create numerical, algebraic or graphical representations of problems and their solutions. They will develop a range of strategies for mental calculation deriving unknown facts from those they know. They will solve word problems about ratio and proportion, use calculators using function keys for reciprocals, squares and powers, manipulate algebraic expressions and use formulae and graphs in solving real-life problems. They will know the properties of triangles, rectilinear figures, circles, cuboids and be able to visualise rotations, transformations, reflections and translations. They will understand and use coordinates and communicate mathematically including using ICT, making use of diagrams and related explanatory text.

Numeracy hour

From September 1999 all primary schools introduced a daily numeracy hour based on the National Numeracy Strategy (NNS) (DfEE 1999c). This sets out in some detail what should be taught at each stage with suggestions for how it might be taught. The strategy suggests that pupils in the primary school should

- have a sense of the size of a number and where it fits into the number system
- know by heart number facts such as number bonds, multiplication tables, doubles and halves
- use what they know to figure out answers mentally
- calculate accurately and efficiently, both mentally and with pencil and paper, drawing on a range of calculation strategies
- recognise when it is appropriate to use a calculator, and be able to do so effectively
- make sense of number problems, including non-routine problems, and recognise the operations needed to solve them
- explain their methods and reasoning using correct mathematical terms
- judge whether their answers are reasonable and have strategies for checking them where necessary
- suggest suitable units for measuring, and make sensible estimates of measurements
- explain and make predictions from the numbers in graphs, diagrams, charts and tables.

(DfEE 1999c: 4)

The framework for teaching suggests that lessons should last about forty-five minutes at Key Stage 1 and fifty to sixty minutes at Key Stage 2. They should be structured to give five to ten minutes of oral work and mental calculation, a main teaching activity of thirty to forty minutes involving both teaching and pupil activity, some of which may be as a whole class, some in groups, in pairs or as individuals and a final plenary session of ten to fifteen minutes to summarise, make links to other work, discuss the next steps and set homework. Oral work should be regarded as an important part of the lesson.

Governors may wonder about the use of calculators. The framework for teaching suggests that they should not be used at Key Stage 1 but at Key Stage 2 pupils should be taught the technical skills of using the calculator. It points out that the calculator 'does offer a unique way of learning about numbers and the number system, place value, properties of numbers, and fractions and decimals' (DfEE 1999c: 8). The advantage of the calculator at an appropriate stage of pupils' learning is that they can be enabled to see number patterns by working out a large number of calculations which would be too time-consuming and tedious to work out otherwise.

Teachers need to look for opportunities for pupils to use their knowledge of number in other work so that they practise using what they know for purposes other than practice. There will be particular opportunities for this in science, technology and probably in geography. In primary schools where teachers teach the whole curriculum it will be easier to see opportunities for practising the skills acquired in one subject in others.

Effective teachers of numeracy

Askew *et al.* (1997) made a study of effective teachers of numeracy defining effectiveness by learning gains. Their findings were as follows:

- Effective teachers had a coherent set of beliefs and understandings about numeracy which underpinned their work. They were clear what it meant to be numerate.
- They believed that being numerate required pupils to have a rich network of connections between different mathematical ideas.
- They believed that almost all pupils could become numerate and that they developed strategies by being challenged to think through explaining, listening and problem solving.
- They had knowledge and awareness of conceptual connections between the areas they taught.
- They were more likely than other teachers to have undertaken substantial in-service training in mathematics.
- They were able in some schools to help colleagues to become more effective.

Science

The *National Curriculum in England: Science* makes the following statement about the importance of science in pupils' education:

> Science stimulates and excites pupils' curiosity about phenomena and events in the world around them. It also satisfies this curiosity with knowledge. Because science links direct practical experience with ideas, it can engage learners at many levels. Scientific method is about developing and evaluating explanations through experimental evidence and modelling. This is a spur to critical and creative thought. Through science, pupils understand how major scientific ideas contribute to technological change – impacting on industry, business and medicine and improving quality of life. Pupils recognise the cultural significance of science and trace its worldwide development. They learn to question and discuss science-based issues that may affect their own lives, the direction of society and the future of the world.
>
> (DfEE 1999c: 1)

Pupils start by learning to observe, explore and ask questions about living things, materials and phenomena and are taught to collect evidence by making observations and measurements when trying to answer a question. They learn to recognise the qualities and needs of living things and how they differ from things which have never been alive. They learn about the characteristics of different materials and study everyday appliances using electricity and study at a simple level forces and motion, light and sound.

Pupils gradually extend their knowledge of living things, materials and phenomena and begin to think about the positive and negative aspects of scientific and technological development. They learn to ask questions which can be investigated scientifically and to carry out more systematic investigations. They learn how to make a fair test by changing one factor in the experiment at a time and observing or measuring the effect. They learn about the life processes in animals such as growth, nutrition and reproduction and about the effect of habitat. They study the human body, its development and how to care for it. They learn about plants, their parts, needs, habitat and methods of reproduction. They learn about the properties of materials and how they can change and how to make an electrical circuit. They develop further their knowledge of force, motion, light and sound and learn about the earth, the sun and the moon.

At the secondary stage pupils learn about scientific inquiry and how to test explanations by using them to make predictions and seeing if the evidence matches the predictions. They learn to collect, use and present evidence using a range of equipment and materials. They learn about human beings as organisms, including nutrition, movement, reproduction, respiration and health. They learn about nutrition, growth, respiration and habitat in plants and learn to classify living things. They learn about solids, liquids and gases, elements, compounds and mixtures, physical and geological changes and chemical reactions. They learn to understand physical processes such as electricity and magnetism, magnetic fields and electromagnets. They learn about forces and motion, force and rotation, force and pressure, light and sound, hearing, vibration and sound. They learn about the solar system and to understand energy sources, energy transfer and conservation of energy.

At Key Stage 4 schools may decide to offer some pupils three separate sciences or combined science. At this stage pupils develop further the learning of Key Stage 3, consider scientific ideas in greater depth and explore how technological advances relate to the scientific ideas underpinning them. They consider the power and limitations of science in addressing industrial, ethical and environmental issues. They use a range of investigative approaches and communicate their findings clearly and precisely. They develop a fuller understanding of life processes.

The survey of standards in secondary education (Ofsted 1999) described above found that science teaching had improved at Key Stage 3 since the previous survey but was about the same at Key Stage 4 and better at post-16.

Art and design

Art and design are concerned with creativity and imagination. Pupils use a variety of materials and processes to communicate ideas in two and three dimensions. They use colour, form, texture, pattern and different materials and processes to communicate their ideas. They evaluate their own work and that of others and study images and artefacts of different genres and styles from different historical, social and cultural contexts, looking at the work of artists, crafts people and designers.

Citizenship

Citizenship is now part of the National Curriculum and it will be a compulsory subject in the secondary school from the year 2002. Primary schools are also expected to teach it at an appropriate level. The advisory group Crick Report (DfEE 1998b) on citizenship identifies three main strands for this:

- Social and moral responsibility – pupils learning self-confidence and socially and morally responsible behaviour.
- Community involvement – pupils learning about becoming involved in the community.
- Political literacy – pupils learning about the institutions, problems and practices of our democracy.

The *National Curriculum in England: Citizenship* (DfEE 1999d: 1) states that 'citizenship gives pupils the knowledge, skills and understanding to play an effective role in society at local, national and international levels. It helps them to become informed, thoughtful and responsible citizens, who are aware of their duties and rights'. In studying citizenship, pupils develop a broad understanding of the rights, responsibilities and duties of citizens. They learn about forms of government, public services, criminal and legal systems. They learn how the public gets information and how opinion is formed and expressed. They evaluate the effectiveness of ways of bringing about change and take part in school and community-based activities and evaluate them.

Design and technology

Design and technology is important because it prepares pupils to participate in the rapidly changing technologies of the future and become autonomous and creative problem-solvers, as individuals and members of a team. Pupils learn to generate ideas, investigating form, function and production processes, planning and making detailed designs taking users' views into account. They learn to work with a range of tools, materials, equipment, components and processes using these with precision, considering social and environmental issues, function and industrial practices as well as aesthetics. They test and evaluate their products.

Geography

Pupils learning geography gradually develop knowledge of places and environments throughout the world, an understanding of maps, and a range of investigative and problem-solving skills both inside and outside the classroom. This is a valuable preparation for adult life and employment. They learn first about the local

environment, observing physical and human features and gradually acquire knowledge of more distant places. They learn to recognise human and physical processes
and to understand the way that people affect their environment and are affected
by it. They begin to appreciate the problems of conflicting demands on the environment. They gradually come to recognise how nations rely on each other. The
study of geography can lead them to think about their own place in the world,
their values, and their rights and responsibilities to other people and the environment.

History

Pupils need to know about the past in Britain and the wider world and develop
an understanding of what past societies were like, how these societies organised
their politics, and what beliefs and cultures influenced people's actions. Pupils
gradually develop a chronological framework for their knowledge of significant
events and people, coming to understand some of the causes and results of events
and making appropriate use of dates and terms. A study of history should help
them to understand today's society and their part in it. Pupils gradually learn to
find evidence, weigh it up and reach their own conclusions, understanding that
there can be different interpretations of events in history.

Information and communication technology (ICT)

Information and communication technology (ICT) is important because in modern
society it is a necessary set of skills for work and other activities. Pupils use ICT
tools to find, explore, analyse, exchange and present information responsibly,
creatively and with discrimination, working with text, images and sound. They
learn to use ICT to organise, classify and present findings, to save information
and retrieve it, structuring, refining and presenting information for different
purposes and audiences. The Internet provides access to ideas and experiences
from a wide range of people, communities and cultures and pupils need to know
how to use this information sensibly. ICT promotes initiative and independent
learning, and pupils gradually learn to make informed judgements about when
and where to use ICT to best effect.

Information and communication technology should be part of every subject in
the curriculum. The Office for Standards in Education survey (Ofsted 1999) found
not only that it was the worst taught subject in the curriculum, but also that 53
per cent of schools did not comply with the requirements of the National
Curriculum and in many schools pupils used information technology facilities in
a fairly mechanical way without thinking critically about their use. This was mainly
due to the fact that teachers themselves were not very confident in using it. It is
clearly an essential set of skills for adult life and governors need to see that teachers
get the necessary training so that they can teach the subject adequately. Governors
also need to be well aware of the extent to which the school has an adequate
supply of up-to-date computers.

Modern foreign languages

Foreign languages are studied at the secondary stage in most schools. Schools must offer at least one of the languages of the European Union.

Pupils learning a foreign language will come to understand and appreciate different countries, cultures, people and communities – and as they do so, begin to think of themselves as citizens of the world as well as of Britain. They gradually develop skill in listening, speaking, reading and writing and in doing so learn about the basic structures of language and how the languages they are studying are both similar to and different from English.

Music

The *National Curriculum in England: Music* (DfEE 1999e: 1) states that 'music is a powerful, unique form of communication that can change the way pupils feel, think and act. It brings together intellect and feeling and enables personal expression, reflection and emotional development'. Music teaching starts with an exploration of sounds and how they are made and can be organised. Pupils learn to recognise and to compose music in different genres and styles and to use appropriate musical vocabulary and notation. They develop the ability to listen and appreciate a wide variety of music and to make judgements about musical quality.

Physical education

Physical education is concerned with developing pupils' physical competence and confidence. Pupils start by learning simple movements and go on to develop precision, control and fluency of movement. The *National Curriculum in England: Physical Education* (DfEE 1999f: 1) states that 'physical education provides opportunities for pupils to be creative, competitive and to face up to different challenges as individuals and in groups and teams. It promotes positive attitudes towards active and healthy lifestyles'. Pupils discuss their own and others' work and use this understanding to improve their performance.

Religious education

Religious education is not part of the National Curriculum but has been a compulsory subject for many years. The programme for religious education for LEA schools is the Agreed Syllabus drawn up by the local Standing Advisory Committee for Religious Education (SACRE). Church schools will have their own Agreed Syllabus.

Most syllabuses for religious education are likely to provide for teaching about Christianity and the Bible and teaching also about other religions practised in Britain.

Parents should be given the opportunity to withdraw their children from religious education if they so wish.

Personal, social and health education

Personal, social and health education is a non-statutory part of the National Curriculum. Secondary schools normally have a programme of personal and social education which may be carried out by form tutors or may also be the responsibility of a group of staff who have a special interest or training in this aspect of curriculum. In the primary school each class teacher has responsibility for personal, social and health education and most of the teaching is likely to be incidental.

David (1993) lists the following objectives of personal, social and health education programmes in secondary schools:

- involving all staff in pastoral as well as academic work
- advising on special educational needs
- dealing with learning difficulties and study skills
- supporting the various welfare needs of pupils
- watching for and attempting to cope with physical, emotional and behavioural problems
- assessing and recording achievement
- liaising with outside agencies
- ensuring order and enforcing discipline
- managing a coordinated programme of tutorial work and personal and social education
- organising and dealing with the administrative tasks of the school
- concern with sport, leisure and community affairs.

David (1993: 191)

Pastoral care might also be seen as involving cooperation with parents and other outside agencies.

Although the list above was compiled with secondary schools in mind, primary school teachers are likely to be dealing with most of the items listed. They are generally in a stronger position to deal with the personal development of pupils because as class teachers they will have much greater contact with a particular group of children than their secondary school colleagues. The problem for them may be that with the pressures created by the literacy and numeracy hours, time for personal, social and health education, other than incidental teaching, may be difficult to find. There are some schools where there is no agreed programme for this work. Governors need to ask questions about this subject and ensure that such a programme exists and is carried out.

Drugs education

It is particularly important that there is an adequate programme which deals with health issues and such matters as diet and drugs. It is thought that between 30 and 40 per cent of pupils of school age have experimented with drugs and 150 children die annually from solvent-abuse. Teaching about drugs is part of the National Curriculum science programme and is built up through the years of schooling. It includes teaching about the health risks involved in drug-taking.

Some schools also use anecdotal evidence of the way in which drug addiction can lead to crime.

The school needs to have a policy about drug education. Strudwick (1999: 31) suggests that Ofsted looks for policies which contain points such as the following:

- a clear statement of aims and objectives
- how the school will provide drugs education
- drug education in the curriculum, including reference to teaching
- responsibilities of all staff in dealing with related issues
- liaison with other agencies
- resource implications (both materials and staff time)
- how confidential matters will be dealt with
- how parents are involved
- how and when the policy will be monitored and evaluated – and who will undertake this responsibility.

Sex education

Secondary schools must provide sex education which deals with relationships, and includes teaching about HIV and AIDs and other sexually transmitted diseases as well as teaching about reproduction, which is part of the National Curriculum in science. Primary school governors can decide whether or not there should be sex education programme in the school over and above the provision in the National Curriculum and they must decide what should be included. Governors need to ask questions about how any such programme is carried out and whether parents have been made aware of what is involved. In secondary schools, where the sex education programme is compulsory, governors also need to ask questions about the programme, who is involved and the stage of schooling at which different issues are discussed.

Both primary and secondary schools must have a policy for sex education and this should be available free to parents. Sex education at all stages must be provided in a way that encourages pupils to consider morals and the value of family life. Parents have the right to withdraw their children from sex education but not from the areas covered in the National Curriculum.

Careers education

All secondary schools need to provide opportunities for pupils to consider their futures. They should learn about the opportunities available to them through activities such as work experience and industry days or through having an employer as a mentor. The school should liaise with the careers' service to help pupils choose their next steps and plan their post-16 choices with parents and others.

Vocational education

Secondary schools are being encouraged to offer an element of vocational education in Years 10 and 11 and in the sixth form for pupils for whom this would be appropriate. The General National Vocational Qualification (GNVQ) can be offered at foundation, intermediate or advanced level and pupils may study for this instead of certain subjects in the National Curriculum

Post-16 education

There have been a number of recent changes to provision for sixth-formers. These are intended to make the sixth-form curriculum broader and more flexible and to bring it more in line with the curriculum of other European countries. Students will be able to study a mixture of academic and vocational studies if they wish, studying for some A levels or Advanced Subsidiary levels and some GNVQs.

The Qualifications and Curriculum Authority (QCA 1999b) paper on 16–19 education states:

> For courses starting in September 2000, A levels will generally be based on six units of approximately equal size. Three of these will make up an Advanced Subsidiary (AS) course, representative of the first half of an advanced level course of study. The other three will be known as A2, representing the second half. A level and AS courses may be assessed either in stages or at the end of the course.
>
> (QCA 1999b: 5)

From September 2000 students in this age group will also have to take tests in the key skills of communication, application of number and information and communications technology.

Cross-curricular skills and topics

The original version of the National Curriculum included cross-curricular skills, themes and dimensions. When it was revised these were not mentioned but they are now re-emerging in various forms and teachers need to be aware of them and see that they are included in many aspects of curriculum. The original cross-curricular themes were economic and industrial understanding, careers education and guidance, health education, education for citizenship and environmental education.

English, mathematics and ICT are also subjects which should be studied across the curriculum.

Citizenship will be a compulsory part of the National Curriculum for secondary schools from 2001. Environmental education is part of geography and science. Economic and industrial understanding will form part of the curriculum for those who choose business studies and may be part of personal and social education and citizenship. All secondary schools also provide work experience for pupils. Careers education is an important part of education in secondary schools. Health education including education about drugs is part of personal and social education.

Equal opportunities and multicultural education

The dimensions in the original National Curriculum were equal opportunities and multicultural education. All schools need to give thought as to how they are educating pupils in these areas; this applies particularly to single-sex schools and schools where there are few, if any, pupils from ethnic minorities. The need for there to be equal opportunities for all pupils is discussed in more detail in Chapter 10.

Schools which are not racially mixed need to give particular thought to the way in which they prepare pupils for an adult world in which they will meet and possibly work with people of different races. Pupils will come to school with certain attitudes towards people of other races. These attitudes are developed very early, partly from parental example, and schools need to ensure that there is discussion about the importance of seeing people as individuals in their own right, regardless of their colour or gender. It is a good idea for schools in predominantly white areas to make links with schools which are racially mixed so that pupils have the experience of discovering for themselves that people of other races are very similar to themselves in many ways.

There is also an important place for studying other cultures. Religious education in particular gives the opportunity to learn about other religions than Christianity and the school needs to look for other opportunities for learning about other cultures.

Study skills

All schools should be concerned with making children independent learners and therefore need to teach study skills. They include the following skills.

Investigation

Pupils need to learn through observation and experiment. This may involve asking questions, turning to books and other printed material, using a computer and the Internet to find answers. They need to learn how to search for information, using contents lists and indexes. Observing involves learning to use tools which extend the sense such as lenses and microscopes and tools which help measurement such as rulers, clocks, weights and so on.

Classification and analysis

Pupils need to learn about sorting, classifying, ordering, generalising, making and testing hypotheses and problem solving. When material has been collected, learning may involve sorting it out and putting it into order for making generalisations or representing it in some way. Pupils need to learn to use the tools of analysis, such as graphs, databases and spreadsheets.

Evaluation

Pupils need the skills involved in evaluating their own work and that of other people. They should learn gradually to set themselves standards and identify criteria for making judgements.

Problem solving

Pupils need to become problem-solvers in the widest sense. Problem solving is not just something to learn in mathematics, science and technology but in all subjects and in life more generally. There are a range of skills involved in solving problems and teachers need to give pupils guidance and practice in using them. Behaviour can give rise to practice in problem solving. For example, pupils who find it difficult to concentrate for any length of time can be encouraged to see this as a problem to be solved perhaps by setting themselves goals such as working for ten minutes without interrupting anyone else and then gradually increasing this time.

Creativity

Creativity was not one of the skills listed in the early version of the National Curriculum, but it is an important skill area which has a place in the teaching of many subjects. The report of the National Advisory Committee on Creative and Cultural Education (1999: 6) stresses that Britain's economic prosperity and social cohesion depend upon unlocking the potential of every young person:

> By creative education we mean forms of education that develop young people's capacity for original ideas and action: by cultural education we mean forms of education that enable them to engage positively with the growing complexity and diversity of social values and ways of life.

The report stresses that creativity is possible in all areas of human activity and that teachers need to recognise young people's creative capacities and provide the conditions in which they can be realised. All subjects can be the vehicles for pupils' creativity. It is not confined to work in the arts and humanities, important as these are. Creativity in all areas carries with it the idea of action and purpose. It involves encouraging all pupils to believe in their own creative potential, fostering independence of judgement, willingness to take risks and be enterprising and persistent. It involves helping them to find their own creative strengths. Learning to be creative is an essential preparation for adult life.

Cooperative learning

Pupils should learn to work with other people. In adult life a great deal of work involves being part of a team and learning to work with other people. There should be some opportunities for learning the skills involved in this in school. Cooperative learning can be part of work in any subject and may also be a part of extra-curricular activities.

Continuity

A child's education needs to be seen as a continuous process from nursery school to sixth form and beyond. Governors need to question from time to time the arrangements which are being made for continuity at transfer from one phase of education to the next and also from one year to the next and from one teacher to the next in primary schools.

The only statutory requirement is that reports on pupils' achievements must be passed from primary to secondary schools when pupils transfer. The reports must, as a minimum, include the following information:

- The end of Key Stage 1 test results for English and mathematics where these are available.
- The end of Key Stage 1 teacher assessment levels in English, mathematics and science.
- The end of Key Stage 2 test results in English, mathematics and science.
- The end of Key Stage 2 teacher assessment levels in English, mathematics and science.

At transfer stages teachers need to be in touch with the teachers of the previous phase and take seriously the records which are passed on. There is a tendency in the teaching profession to want to start afresh with a new intake of children so as to avoid any prejudice which might arise from previous teachers' views. This can waste a good deal of work and knowledge which has been built up by previous teachers.

It can be helpful at the transfer from primary to secondary school to give a questionnaire to pupils at the end of the intake year asking them among other questions about whether work done in the primary school has been repeated and if so, in what subjects. Some repetition will be inevitable, especially in subjects like mathematics where teachers will need to revise previous work to ensure that all pupils have understood it, but this kind of questioning can lead to teachers making better use of the information coming from the primary schools. A questionnaire which includes a question about repeated subject material is given in the Appendix.

Part of looking at continuity will be what is passed on from year to year and the kinds of records which one teacher passes on to the next. At the reception class stage in the primary school there may be records from nursery schools or classes and also information from parents.

Homework

It is now government policy that all schools should give pupils homework. This would involve only a small amount for the youngest children where it might involve reading to a parent or family member but gradually build up as children moved through each phase of schooling.

A study by Weston (1999) for the Office for Standards in Education of schools where homework was used effectively involved a telephone survey of 368 primary and secondary schools and case study visits to 29 schools where teachers, parents and pupils were interviewed. She found that primary schools recognised the importance of the parents' role and some made homework voluntary. The kind of homework given at this stage involved such activities as learning tables and spellings, reading to someone in the family and completing project work begun in school. Some primary schools provided guidelines and workshops for parents on helping children with reading, writing and spelling.

The schools in the study felt that preplanning homework helped teachers with continuity and progression, appropriateness of tasks for children, consistency of approach and gave a clear framework with explicit goals. Parents appreciated the information provided on what was to be done. There was more preplanning in primary than secondary schools where some teachers felt that planning might prevent good matching of work to the class in question.

The study found that homework was more likely to be associated with improvements in achievement when there was rapid and regular feedback. It found some indicators of good practice were integrating homework and classwork, tailoring homework to individual learning, building a partnership with parents and working to develop independent learning.

The hidden curriculum

All schools have a hidden curriculum. One part of this might be called an inferred curriculum, learning which is inferred from the way pupils are treated and the behaviour which teachers feel to be acceptable. A good deal of this learning is never made explicit but pupils learn what is and is not acceptable from their teachers' reactions to them. The values that the headteacher and staff hold will be expressed in the way they behave to each other and to the pupils. When a new teacher joins the staff he or she has to learn 'how we do things here' by observing and listening rather than by being told, although there will be some values made explicit. Governors too have to observe and listen in order to pick up the value system operating in the school. Much can be learned from observing how teachers deal with pupils.

There is also a curriculum that is more hidden than this, which is never made explicit and rarely talked about. Do pupils get the idea that English and mathematics are more important than other subjects? Do they believe that teachers favour boys more than girls or vice versa? Have pupils learned that it does not pay to finish work quickly because they simply get more of the same? Governors will pick up this kind of information from looking and listening to what happens in the school.

Assessment

Assessment takes place at a variety of levels in schools. It may be formative, taking place while the work is in hand, or summative, taking place when the work is completed. Both types of assessment are necessary but formative assessment is likely to make the greater contribution to the pupil's learning.

The national tests and teacher assessment which grade pupils as being at particular levels of attainment were described in Chapter 2. Thus 7 year olds are expected to reach level 2 in English and mathematics and 11 year olds, level 4, while 14 year olds should reach between levels 5 and 6. Teachers also assess pupils according to these levels and there are published guidelines which tell them what to expect at each level.

Governors are responsible for seeing that all these assessments are carried out and for ensuring that the results of tests and assessments are reported to parents and published in the school prospectus and the annual report to parents.

A report by Ofsted (1999) suggests that in most subjects in the secondary school, most teachers make too little use of assessment to help pupils to learn. They tend to grade work but not to use the information sufficiently in planning new work.

A report by the Assessment Reform Group (1999: 4) suggests that schools could make much more use of assessment in helping pupils to achieve. It needs to be designed to help learning rather than as a means of grading pupils by comparison with each other. They quote an article by Black and Wiliam (1998) who reviewed research into assessment and learning and found that assessment improved learning where the following factors operated:

- provision of effective feedback to pupils
- active involvement of pupils in their own learning
- adjusting teaching to take account of the results of assessment
- a recognition of the profound influence assessment has on the motivation and self-esteem of pupils, both of which are crucial influences on learning
- the need for pupils to be able to assess themselves and understand how to improve.

They also found that teachers had a tendency to assess the quantity of work and its presentation rather than the quality of learning it represented.

A school assessment policy should stress the positive role which assessment can play in pupils' learning. The school needs to have a common approach to assessment and marking work and the criteria used need to be clear to pupils and their parents. Some schools also grade work for effort as well as content and many teachers make use of comments designed to contribute to the pupil's self-esteem where possible and to help the pupil to improve the work. Comments may also reflect the use of target setting for individual pupils.

School records

Schools must keep records of the achievement and progress of all pupils. These are important for ensuring continuity and should form part of the assessment process and inform teaching. Records must be made available to parents who ask to see them and teachers must be able to substantiate anything they record. Schools need to have a policy about what should be recorded so that the records of all teachers have some similarity although teachers may want to keep their own unofficial records as well as the main school record. Information about children transferring to another school must be passed on.

In addition to the records kept by teachers, secondary schools are expected to work with pupils to keep a record of personal achievement. These are intended to record not only achievement and progress in school work and behaviour but also out-of-school achievements which are important to the pupil. Time needs to be given to completing these records on a regular basis and as pupils reach school leaving age, a summary record is made that can be shown to employers or those interviewing for places in further or higher education. A similar record might be made by older pupils in the primary school.

Questions to consider

1   Is our school teaching all the National Curriculum subjects effectively?
2   Do we have whole-school policies for literacy and numeracy?
3   Are all the teachers aware of these policies? Do they carry them out?
4   (Primary schools) What effect are the literacy and numeracy hours having on our SATs results?
5   (Secondary schools) Are English and mathematics teachers aware of the work done in the primary schools in the literacy and numeracy hours?
6   Is religious education taught effectively?
7   What skills are being taught through the National Curriculum? Are pupils acquiring study skills and problem-solving skills?
8   What is being taught through personal, social and health education?
9   Do we have an assessment policy in place and is it being implemented?

Chapter 9

Responsibility for staff

Governors have the following duties in relation to staffing:

- They can decide the number of staff the school should employ and can decide whether to replace a member of staff who leaves.
- They are responsible for staff discipline and may appoint, dismiss and suspend staff.
- They can make a range of decisions about pay for teaching staff and can decide the grade at which non-teaching staff are appointed.
- They must have arrangements for hearing staff grievances.
- They must keep to relevant parts of employment law and may have to appear before an industrial tribunal to defend their actions.
- They are responsible for seeing that appraisal of teaching staff takes place.

Relationships with staff

It is important that governors have good relationships with staff so that when difficulties arise they can be resolved amicably. Creese (1995: 28) studied the relationships of governors and staff in eight schools. Teachers and governors identified the following as leading to good relationships between staff and governors:

- frequent and close contact
- mutual understanding and respect
- openness and honesty
- good communication
- trust
- common aims
- school ethos.

Teachers in this study referred to 'supportive governors'.

Good relationships are also enhanced by such schemes as governor links with classes or departments, joint working parties of staff and governors, staff presentations at governors' meetings, use of governors' expertise in school, staff in-service on the role of governors and governors' visits to the school. There is also a place for social occasions at which staff and governors come together.

Teachers' qualifications and conditions of service

To teach in a maintained school in England and Wales, a teacher must have qualified teacher status (QTS). This is normally obtained either through a recognised course of teacher training taken after a degree is obtained (Postgraduate Certificate of Education – PGCE) or through training in which a degree in education is taken concurrently with training for teaching. Teachers can also become qualified through the employment-based Licensed Teacher Scheme or by an overseas qualification which is recognised in England and Wales.

When governors have chosen a teacher they wish to appoint, the LEA must check that the person meets the qualifications and health regulations. The LEA will also check List 99, which is a list held by the Department for Education and Employment of teachers who are barred from teaching or other work involving contact with children. They may also arrange a police check of criminal records. If there are any circumstances which raise doubts about the appointment, the LEA will ask governors to reconsider their decision.

The employment of teachers is governed by national regulations set out in DfEE (1999b) *Circular 12/99*. Teachers must be available for work on 195 days in the year of which 5 are days set aside for in-service training within the school. They must be available for 1,265 hours, which is the equivalent of a 37 hour week, and cannot be compelled to work for longer than this at school or to take part in supervision of school meals. In practice virtually all teachers work longer hours than these, putting in many hours at home as well as at school. These are not counted as part of the 1,265 hours.

Teachers who are pregnant with less than one year's continuous service at the start of the eleventh week before the expected date of birth are entitled to up to eighteen weeks' maternity leave. This is unpaid leave with only the financial entitlement to statutory maternity pay. Those with at least one year's continuous service are entitled to up to eighteen weeks' paid maternity leave. Two years' continuous service entitles the teacher to up to twenty-nine weeks' paid maternity leave.

Pay

Teachers' rates of pay are fixed by law and governing bodies must keep to the rules. They can decide on the point on the pay spine at which the headteacher and deputies are appointed, based on the minimum dependent on the size of the school. The pay of other teachers is based on a points scale in which points are awarded for a good honours degree and relevant experience. Governors may also award points to teachers who take on extra responsibility, show excellence in teaching, are specially qualified for special needs teaching or have posts which are hard to fill. Governors are required to review the salary of every teacher each September.

Governors decide whether the headteacher and deputies should have a pay increase by moving one or more points up the pay scale. This must be decided on the basis of the achievement of targets previously agreed.

Governors may also put forward the names of exceptionally able teachers for the grade of Advanced Skills Teacher (AST). These are teachers who do not wish to leave the classroom for management posts in a school, but want to progress within their profession. To achieve this grade a teacher must pass a national assessment. He or she will then have additional duties concerned with the development of other teachers, particularly with newly qualified teachers during their induction year. Such teachers will then progress beyond the top of the normal salary scale.

Governors also decide the pay of support and administrative staff when they are appointed, within the scales laid down.

Performance management and appraisal

Research suggests that there is a gap between what school management thinks is happening in classrooms and what is actually happening. Some schools are also coasting, perhaps relying on previous good performance and a preponderance of able children to keep their results above the national average. There is a need for greater management of teachers' performance. There has been a requirement for appraisal systems in schools for some time but pressures of work have meant that appraisal has not always been carried out in a satisfactory way.

From September 2000 schools have to have a system of appraisal under which each teacher is appraised annually and three to six targets or objectives are agreed. These should be 'challenging', clear and concise but flexible as they may need to change during the year and should cover pupil progress based on prior attainment and the personal development of the teacher and should link to the school development plan. The school should have an agreed appraisal form and there should be agreement about classroom observation and the way in which progress towards targets will be monitored.

Governors should receive regular reports from the headteacher on how the appraisal system is working. Appraisal applies to all qualified teachers on contracts of at least a year full-time or on 40 per cent or more of full-time.

All teachers who reach the top of the salary scale may opt to be considered for assessment to go on to a further scale which will give them an immediate rise of £2,000. The outcome of appraisal will help to determine this. Teachers have to apply to go above the threshold and will be assessed by the headteacher, where appropriate by their team leader and an external assessor on their professionalism, thinking, planning, leading and relating to others. Classroom climate will be considered, taking into account order, participation, standards achieved, clarity, support for pupils, fairness, safety, the working environment and the interest aroused in the pupils. Governors will have the oversight of this programme.

A governing body should have a pay policy which states the aims of pay and is a statement of general principles. It should cover support staff as well as teaching staff. Possible elements of such a policy are as follows:

- the principles underlying the policy and its aims
- a statement of commitment to equal opportunities
- a statement on appraisal and its relation to pay
- the need for job descriptions for all posts
- procedures for decisions on pay for teaching and non-teaching staff

- policy on acting allowances e.g. acting headteacher(s)
- procedures for the annual review of headteacher and deputy headteacher(s) salaries
- arrangements for appeals.

Appointment of staff

Headteacher and deputy headteacher appointments must be nationally advertised and while the governing body can delegate interviewing to a selection panel, the appointment must be ratified by the whole governing body. The chief education officer or his or her representative has a right to attend relevant meetings of the selection panel to offer advice but not to vote. Governors have a duty to consider this advice before appointing. If there is no decision the post must be readvertised. The LEA must appoint the candidate recommended by the governors unless he or she does not meet the legal requirements on qualifications and health or is on List 99.

The chief education officer or his or her representative and the headteacher also have a right to attend selection panels for other staff. A copy of the job specification must be sent to the LEA, which may put forward names of qualified candidates whom they would like the governing body to consider. These may be teachers who have become redundant at other schools. Posts must be advertised unless the governors decide to appoint someone put forward by the LEA or an internal candidate. Generally speaking it is wise to advertise all posts since making an internal appointment without considering the merits of the internal candidate in comparison with those of external candidates may mean that the school is not getting the best appointment. On the other hand, an internal candidate who is not successful in competition may find this distressing.

Before the advertisement is drawn up, the selection panel should set out a job description which gives details of the tasks which the person appointed would be required to undertake and a person description setting out the qualifications, experience and interests which the panel would be looking for in making the appointment. Generally speaking, the headteacher is the best person to do this but the governors concerned should agree both job description and person specification. These lead to a statement of further particulars about the school and the post, which will be sent to candidates writing for application forms. The panel may also decide whether to use a local authority form, one devised by themselves or simply to ask for letters of application. There is much to be said for having an application form. This provides the same information about every candidate. In a letter of application a candidate may choose to hide some information.

It is a good idea to ask for specific questions to be answered in making an application. This again gives comparable information about candidates and ensures that what is said in the application is relevant to the post in question.

Discrimination

There is very clear legislation against discriminating by gender, race or disability and governors need to be careful not to discriminate indirectly by, for example, making a blanket requirement for full-time work which may discriminate against women who have greater home responsibilities than men. Disability discrimination requires governors to consider whether it would be possible to employ a disabled person if 'reasonable adjustments' were made to their working environment.

It is a good idea to keep a record of the balance of men and women selected for interview and appointed over a period; in a school where there are usually a fair number of candidates from ethnic minorities keep a note of how many are interviewed and how many appointed.

Short-listing

Once a post has been advertised and applications received, it is the practice in education to obtain confidential references from referees given by the candidates. If there are many applications, someone may go through the list taking out those who are clearly unsuitable by reason of experience and qualifications and write to the referees of the rest. It is wise to ask specific questions of referees and to suggest that they use a particular form of words of recommendation. For example, they may be asked to say whether they strongly support the candidate, support him or her, support with reservations (stated) or do not support. This gives comparable information for all candidates although referees do not always follow this instruction.

Short-listing those to be interviewed should be done by a panel, not an individual, and should be based on objective criteria, derived from the job description and the person specification and weighed against the information on the application form and the statements made by the referees. There is much to be said for having a pro-forma for the short-listing panel on which to score each candidate and comment against criteria such as qualifications, experience, skills/abilities, personal qualities and job-specific requirements. The same pro-forma can be used for the interview itself. The short-list can then be arrived at by a mixture of agreed scoring and discussion.

Mayhill secondary school was appointing a new deputy head. Once the short-list had been drawn up and the candidates invited, the panel that the governors had appointed had to agree on the selection process they wished to use. They decided to set up various ways of finding out about the candidates in addition to interviewing them.

When the candidates arrived in the school on the first day of a two-day selection process, they met the head and chair of governors and were given a tour of the school by sixth-formers. They then did an in-tray exercise which involved writing responses to a series of problems which had been taken from ones which the school had actually met. In the afternoon each candidate was asked to present a problem which he or she had encountered in school and lead a discussion about it with the other candidates. This gave the opportunity for a number of governors who were not involved in interviewing to act as observers and score the candidates on their presentation and their ability to lead discussion.

The morning of the second day was devoted to interviews with each candidate meeting four panels of two governors. The panels included a teacher governor and the headteacher. Each panel had a specific interviewing task. One asked questions about management, another about curriculum, a third about personal and social education and a fourth about staff development. Questions were agreed beforehand and each panel was aware of the questions the others were asking. This did not preclude interviewers from using the candidates' application forms as a starting point for a question. At lunchtime the interviewers met and decided to call three of the six candidates for the final interview in the afternoon.

The final interviews were with a panel of four governors, including the headteacher, the chair of governors, the chair of the personnel committee and one other governor. The panel then chose the final candidate who was then presented to the full governing body, who had to ratify the appointment.

Making the appointment

It is valuable in making the appointment for a headteacher or deputy head to find various ways of involving governors in making assessments, so that most of them have had a chance to make a judgement about the candidates. It can also be helpful to get some feedback from other members of staff on their reaction to the candidates and in secondary schools with a sixth form, from the older pupils.

Interview panels should be kept small and there is much to be said for having more than one interview for all posts. Different interviewers can draw out different information and it is much better to use all the time the candidates are in the school in finding out about them than leaving them sitting doing nothing. It is customary in making such appointments to keep candidates waiting until a decision has been made, rather than interviewing them and letting them go, to be contacted by telephone or letter at a later stage. This is partly because a number of people have to agree about an appointment and it may be difficult to assemble them again. It is also because the arrangements whereby teachers normally leave a post at the end of a term and must give notice by a certain date means that those seeking to move need to know very quickly if they are to be offered the post as all the interviews will be taking place around the same time.

In interviewing it is generally more useful to ask questions about what the candidate has actually done than it is to ask about how he or she would deal with a hypothetical situation, although there is a place for some questions of this kind. Interviewers should be careful not to ask questions about religious affiliation (except in a church school), political views or trade union membership. They should also avoid asking female candidates questions which they would not ask of male candidates. Similarly black candidates should not be asked questions which would not be asked of white candidates. Where disabled candidates are concerned, the only criterion is whether the person will be able to teach effectively given appropriate support.

Other questions to avoid are those likely to produce one word answers, except where you are checking facts, and leading questions. For example 'I think schools today need more discipline. Do you agree?' This places candidates in a difficult position. Should they agree whatever their own opinion or be honest and disagree whatever they really think?

Questions which governors need to ask themselves about the candidates are as follows:

- What sort of a relationship is this teacher likely to have with pupils?
  There is a great deal of evidence to suggest that unless a teacher has a good relationship with pupils their learning is likely to suffer.
- Has this teacher a clear idea of how he/she will enable pupils to learn?
  Descriptions of work the teacher has undertaken should give a good idea of how he or she teaches.
- Is this teacher likely to communicate well with pupils?
  If a teacher can communicate well with an interviewing panel and perhaps evoke some excitement about what he or she is saying, that teacher is likely to be able to enthuse pupils.
- Is this teacher a good organiser and planner?
  Good teaching depends upon good organisation. A teacher needs to be able to plan ahead. Questioning should elicit the ways in which the teacher plans and organises work.
- Does this teacher evaluate his/her work?
  Good teachers are self-critical. It should be possible to gather information about this from questioning.
- Will this teacher be able to deal with the pastoral aspects of the teacher's work in a satisfactory way?
  In a secondary school most teachers will be form tutors and all teachers find themselves advising and counselling pupils from time to time. Primary school teachers need to be sensitive and sympathetic to children.

Questioning should reveal attitudes towards children and young people.

Where the post is at a senior level, interviewers might consider the following:

- Is this teacher likely to make good relationships with adults as well as pupils?
  Good management, like good teaching, is dependent upon relationships.
- Has this teacher the necessary skills for working with adults? Could he or she lead a group, counsel individuals, praise and encourage, elicit ideas, deal honestly with failure and so on.
- Has this teacher skill in setting goals and targets and planning and organising to achieve them?
- Has this teacher skill in analysing and solving problems?
- Has this teacher skill in dealing with administration and organisation as it affects the post in question?

It is not a good idea to discuss candidates between the interviews but panel members should make their own notes and score the candidates against a previously agreed schedule. At the end of the interviewing process, it is helpful to ask whether there are any candidates whom members of the panel consider to be unsuitable. This often eliminates some people and leaves for discussion only those who are possibilities. The panel can then discuss the strengths and weaknesses of the remaining candidates using all the information available from the various selection activities that have been used. It can be useful at this stage to ask panel members for their order of preference. This sometimes shortens discussion because everyone may be agreed on the person at the top of the list. On other occasions there is considerable difference and discussion needs to go on until there is agreement. If agreement cannot be reached or if the panel feel that no candidate is ready for the appointment then they may decide to readvertise.

Once agreement has been reached the successful candidate should be called back and offered the job. It is important to be careful about what is said at this stage as it can have a legal standing. If, for example, there is discussion about the point on the pay spine the person will start at, this can be upheld if there is later dissension from it. There may also be some discussion about responsibilities which may be queried at a later date. Interviewing panels need to be very clear about this kind of detail before they offer the post to a candidate.

Where posts other than headships and deputy headships are concerned, it is a good idea to set up a teaching situation for each candidate, so that such things as ability to relate to pupils and skill in exposition and questioning can be judged. Candidates will need to know about this in advance with details of the group they will be teaching so that they can prepare properly. This again can involve governors and appropriate senior members of staff in observation.

After the interviews are over the members of the panel should be prepared to give some feedback to the unsuccessful candidates. This should be discussed and someone briefed to talk to each person giving information about the reaction of the panel and suggesting areas in which he or she might develop further.

Finally governing bodies should from time to time ask the headteacher for reports on how the teachers appointed are working out in practice. How far was the impression gained in the process of selection borne out in their work in post? Very few schools do this but it can be a salutary way of making judgements about the effectiveness of the selection process.

Staff development

Governors are responsible for seeing that staff have the opportunity to develop the skills and knowledge they need to do their work. Education is something that does not stand still and teachers continue to need in-service education throughout their working lives. Non-teaching staff may also need opportunities to enhance their skills and this is also true of teaching support staff. Each school is allowed five days annually for staff training and governors need to be aware of the way these days are being used as well as noting the courses that staff have attended. In many schools, governors who are free to do so are often invited to join in and this is a good opportunity to learn about the work of the teachers.

Induction of newly qualified teachers

Teachers who qualified after May 1999 have to complete an induction period of three school terms or the equivalent in order to work in maintained schools. The DfEE *Circular 5/99* on this provision states that:

> The induction period will combine an individualised programme of monitoring and support which provides opportunities for NQTs [Newly Qualified Teachers] to develop further their knowledge, skills and achievements in relation to the standards for the award of QTS [Qualified Teacher Status], with an assessment of their performance.
>
> (DfEE 1999a)

When appointing a newly qualified teacher, governors have to ensure that the school is able to provide a support programme. NQTs are also entitled to a teaching programme which is not more than 90 per cent of the pupil–teacher contact time normally worked by teachers in the school. If the school is very small, the provision of induction may require some experience in another school.

Each NQT should be given a mentor, who will normally be the teacher's line manager or a senior member of the staff. In small primary schools this will probably be the headteacher. The induction programme should include opportunities for the teacher to observe other teachers in action and opportunities to be observed by his or her mentor. There should also be discussion of the teacher's work and short, medium and long term objectives should be agreed and progress towards them monitored. Written records should be kept of discussions of objectives agreed and of progress. The teacher concerned should be actively involved in this and encouraged to evaluate his or her own work. There should be a meeting between the NQT and his or her mentor at least termly.

At the end of the induction period a decision must be reached as to whether or not the teacher has satisfactorily completed the induction and the appropriate form should be completed and sent to the LEA. Teachers who fail the induction period may appeal but there is no second chance.

Training for headteachers

Headteachers will increasingly be qualified for their role by the National Professional Qualification for Headteachers (NPQH) and a national training centre for headteachers is being set up. This will give governors assurance that newly appointed headteachers have the necessary management skills and knowledge. Governors will also be concerned with other members of staff, usually deputy headteachers or senior teachers, who wish to qualify themselves for headship.

Discipline of staff

Governors are responsible for setting out disciplinary rules and procedures for staff, such as grievance and complaints procedures. These must be made known to staff. Part-time as well as full-time staff are entitled to full employment protection rights.

The day-to-day discipline of staff is the responsibility of the headteacher but governors become involved if a member of staff needs to be suspended or dismissed. The governors and the headteacher both have the power to suspend a teacher or any other staff member on full pay. Governors and headteacher must inform each other in a case of suspension and the LEA must also be informed. Only the governing body has the power to end a suspension.

The power of dismissal rests with the governing body and may be delegated to a committee of three or more governors, the Staff Dismissal Committee. The LEA must be informed immediately but the person concerned must be informed about the opportunity to appeal against the decision before it is communicated to the LEA. The appeal will be to the Staff Dismissal Appeals Committee which must comprise at least three members who have not been involved in the original dismissal decision. The staff member concerned is entitled to bring a 'friend' (usually a union representative) to any disciplinary hearing. The LEA must dismiss the employee within fourteen days of being notified of the governors' decision unless the person concerned has resigned in the mean time.

While a few cases where dismissal is required may be straightforward, as when someone has committed a crime, the more difficult case for the governors is that of the teacher or other member of staff who is under-performing. The first requirement is to try to define the standard which would be considered acceptable and to make the person concerned aware of this. The headteacher then needs to see that a programme of support for the person is set in place. In the case of a teacher this may involve the headteacher and more senior members of the staff observing the teacher in action, arranging a programme of in-service training for the person concerned and perhaps inviting an adviser from outside the school to give an opinion and suggest ways forward. A period must be agreed during which the staff member must show improvement. At the end of this time if there has been no improvement, a final warning may be given that failure to improve will lead to dismissal. This must be given in writing.

One of the problems about this procedure is that under-performing teachers tend to make some improvement while the pressure is on but the improvement fades once it ceases. In the long run governors have to decide whether the pupils are really losing out because of the problems this teacher poses.

Staff who feel they have been unfairly treated may have recourse to an industrial tribunal which deals with cases concerned with such issues as unfair dismissal and redundancy disputes, race, sex and disability discrimination, maternity rights, trade union rights, health and safety rights, unfair deduction from pay and breaches of employment contract. In cases brought by teachers at maintained schools the teacher is the Applicant and the governing body the Respondent, even though the LEA is legally the employer. Governors therefore need to be very careful in dealing with cases which could result in a tribunal hearing.

Redundancy and retirement

Governors are now responsible for keeping within their budget and this means that some schools will find on occasion there is a fall in pupil numbers and that staff need to be made redundant because otherwise the budget will not cover the salary bill. There may also be situations where a school decides to cease to offer a particular course or there are too few pupils choosing a course and this too may make staff redundant.

In some cases it may be possible for teachers who are nearing retirement to leave early. In other cases governors will have to plan redundancies of staff in mid-career. There is a risk of unfair dismissal claims from teachers made redundant in this way and governors need to have a clear procedure for dealing with the situation. Potter and Smellie (1997: 99) writing of claims for unfair dismissal suggest that a tribunal is likely to ask questions such as the following:

1   Were the employees warned as soon as possible and consulted as to the best means of reducing staff levels with minimum hardship?
2   Were the selection criteria chosen objectively and applied fairly?
3   Was the possibility of transfer to other work investigated thoroughly?

It is important to warn staff as soon as possible that redundancies are being considered, giving the reasons for the redundancies, the number of people likely to be made redundant, how they will be selected and when and how dismissal will be carried out and the redundancy package they can expect. Selection criteria should then be agreed. A pool of people who could be made redundant should be defined and information about the possibilities should be given to those likely to be involved at a meeting and also in writing. The criteria should be set out in writing and might include such factors as:

•   skills or qualifications
•   attendance or disciplinary records
•   length of service
•   standard of performance
•   flexibility.

All the proposals should be agreed with the appropriate trade unions and professional organisations. It is important that the selection criteria are employed fairly and proposals should be double-checked. Consideration should also be given to alternative possibilities for those concerned. Could a post be made part-time instead of full-time, for example? Could someone whose post is no longer needed function in another capacity? Can the LEA suggest any possible posts for which the people concerned could apply? An employee who accepts an alternative post is not entitled to redundancy payment but has a statutory right to a trial period of four weeks in the new job. If the employee decides during this period not to continue with the new job then he or she can accept dismissal with a redundancy payment.

Teachers' pensions

A person nearing retirement age may wish to retire early or may choose retirement if the school is faced with the need to reduce staff. Teachers may retire at 60 and receive a pension from the Teachers' Superannuation Scheme (TSS) or have a personal pension. If the teacher is under 60 and wishes to retire early under the TSS, the employer (whether the LEA or, in the case of voluntary schools, the governors), must certify to the Secretary of State that the teacher is being made redundant or is retiring in the interests of the efficient discharge of the employer's functions.

Pensions are calculated on the number of years served. It is possible for extra years' benefits to be awarded to teachers retiring early. There will be an authority which decides that this shall be done and an authority which pays. For maintained schools the governing body is the deciding authority and the LEA the compensating authority. Governors should consult the LEA before making any such arrangements as it is possible that the LEA will wish to recoup the payments from the school's budget. Pensions will be calculated so that the cost of each pension to the Teachers' Superannuation Scheme is equivalent to the expected cost if the pension had been paid in full from age 60.

Stress

Teachers experience many of the causes of stress. There are increasing pressures on the teaching profession year by year and sometimes the demands are conflicting. The demands for ever better standards of achievement from pupils and the degree of inspection which schools now experience are all stressful. Although teachers get longer holidays than most other workers, they generally work very long hours during the term. In primary schools, the advent of the literacy and mathematics hours has required much preparation for each day's work. In secondary schools the need to improve examination results year on year has also been stressful.

Governors need to be sympathetic to the pressures on teachers and to consider new developments from teachers' points of view. Governors also need to be on the look out for bullying of staff, which is another cause of stress. Signs of stress include increases in sickness absence, tensions and conflicts, and loss of motivation by staff.

Stress can be avoided by ensuring that the tasks demanded of staff are reasonable and within their ability, that there is good communication, that responsibilities are clearly defined and that there are good training opportunities. Staff also need to feel that what they do is appreciated. It is important that the head and senior staff praise their colleagues when praise is due and that governors make a point of writing to congratulate staff on such things as test and examination results, good school productions and activities of various kinds.

Questions to consider

1 How well do we know the school staff?
2 How much do the staff know about the governors? Do they see us as supportive of their work?
3 Have we agreed objectives with our headteacher and deputy head(s)?
4 How many of our staff are being paid above the threshold? Is this having any effect on staff relationships?

5 How well is our appraisal programme working? What do the teachers think of it?

6 Have we a good system for making appointments which involves most governors from time to time?

7 Do we ever consider how good the people we appoint turn out to be? Was the impression we gained at interview a fair one?

8 Do we have a good staff development programme?

9 Is our induction programme for NQTs working out well?

10 Have we an appropriate organisation to deal with staff discipline and, if necessary, dismissal?

11 Would we know what to do if we were faced with the need to make someone redundant?

12 Are any members of our staff suffering from stress or from bullying? How will we know this?

Chapter 10

Responsibility for pupils

Admissions

There are clear regulations about the admission of pupils to schools. Each school has a standard admission number (SAN) based on the school's physical capacity and parents have a right to have their child admitted to the school of their choice unless the standard admission number has been reached or the school selects some or all its pupils by ability or aptitude.

For community schools and voluntary-controlled schools the LEA is the admission authority and must publish admission criteria by which decisions are made when more parents wish their children to go to a school than there are places for them. Foundation schools and voluntary-aided schools are the admission authority and must do likewise. Admissions criteria must be clear, objective and fair and compatible with equal opportunities legislation.

Schools may in some cases choose to select a proportion of their pupils by ability and in the case of specialist schools, up to 10 per cent of their pupils by aptitude. Other criteria may include such things as having siblings in the school, geographical proximity or medical reasons. Church schools may wish to give preference to children whose parents are members of their particular denomination. Applicants may be refused if their admission would impair the delivery of efficient education at the school or the efficient use of resources and, in the case of a selective school, if the applicant does not meet the criteria for admission. LEAs must consult governors about admission arrangements. If there is a waiting list the school must make it clear how children will be ranked. There is pressure from government now to make coordinated arrangements for admission within an area so that parents do not experience applying to several schools and ending up with no place for their child.

LEAs and governors of foundation and voluntary-aided schools must have an appeals procedure which can be used by parents who have been unsuccessful in getting their child into the school of their choice and parents must be told of this when they are informed that there is not a place for their child in the school they have chosen. The appeals procedure involves having an appeals committee whose decisions are binding on both the LEA and the school. Where parents are dissatisfied with the decision of an appeal, they may take their case to the Ombudsman if they think there has been poor administration.

Discipline

Governors have a duty to draw up a statement about discipline in consultation with parents. According to the DfEE (1998d) the statement should include:

- the ethos of the school, offering a clear and defensible set of values and making clear the boundaries of acceptable behaviour
- the school's moral code
- positive and constructive rules of conduct
- the rewards and punishments to be fairly and consistently applied.

The Advisory Centre for Education (1998) states that:

> The head must determine measures (which may include the making of rules and provision for enforcing them) to be taken with a view to:
>
> (i)   promoting among pupils, self-discipline and proper regard for authority;
> (ii) encouraging good behaviour and respect for others on the part of pupils – the School Standards and Framework Act introduces bullying into legislation for the first time by adding that measures should prevent 'all forms of bullying among pupils';
> (iii) securing that the standard of behaviour of pupils is acceptable; and
> (iv) otherwise regulating the conduct of pupils.
> (Advisory Centre for Education 1998: 52)

Ideally a policy should have a section that is specifically for pupils which sets out what is expected of them in the classroom and about the school. This section constitutes the rules of the school. Teachers will have rules for behaviour in the classroom. The policy will also set out rewards and sanctions. Headteachers should make this policy public at least annually to parents, pupils and all staff.

Detention is now legally allowed without parental consent but parents should be given twenty-four hours notice of a detention.

Exclusions

The ultimate sanction available to a school is exclusion, which may be for a given period of not more than fifteen days in a given term, or permanent. Only the headteacher can exclude a pupil and parents should be informed immediately of the reason for the exclusion, its duration and their right to make representations to the governing body. If the exclusion is permanent, parents must be told that they have a right of appeal to the LEA.

The headteacher must tell the governing body and the LEA straight away of exclusions of more than five days in any one term and of any exclusions which would involve the loss of the opportunity to take a public examination. He or she must give the reasons for the exclusion. The governing body must consider any parent representation and can reinstate a pupil if it so decides. The LEA and the parents must be informed when this happens and where the governors decide not to reinstate, reasons must be given for this decision. The LEA can also require a school to reinstate a pupil although it must consult the governors before doing so. The governing body has a right of appeal against the LEA's direction to reinstate a pupil who has been permanently excluded.

Governors' panels hearing exclusion cases should include at least three governors who have not been involved in the original decision to exclude and their decision may have to be justified to an appeal panel.

From September 1994 governing bodies, LEAs and independent appeal panels have had to act within set time limits when considering permanent exclusion. At county and church controlled schools the LEA has twenty days from the date when the parents were told of the exclusion, to decide whether or not a permanent exclusion should stand, taking into account any representations by parents. The LEA must within fifteen days give the governors the chance to express their views.

The government is anxious for schools to reduce the number of children who are permanently excluded from schools and LEA targets may well include a target for this reduction.

Truancy

There is a government target to reduce truancy by one-third by the year 2002 and this too is likely to feature in LEA targets.

The governors of a school are responsible for seeing that there is a register for admissions and registers for attendance. Under the Education (Pupils' Attendance Records) Regulations (DES 1991) schools must show in their attendance records whether the absence of a pupil was authorised or unauthorised. The rates of authorised and unauthorised absence have to be published in the school prospectus and the annual report to parents. Handwritten registers must be kept in ink. Computerised registers must be printed out at least once a month and the printouts bound into an annual volume each year. The registers must be made available to inspectors and to anyone authorised by the Secretary of State or the LEA.

Schools are using various strategies to try to reduce truancy. Some are including it as a topic in their personal and social education schemes. There are schools where special care is taken to provide opportunities for pupils who have been absent to catch up on their work. Some schools have developed panels of pupils to help to combat truancy. Governors of a school where truancy is high might ask questions about what was being done to change this.

Truancy is important not only because pupils who truant are missing out on their education, but also because truants tend to get into trouble and are responsible for a good deal of crime and vandalism. In some areas the police have powers to return truants to school and are concerned about the social problems that such pupils produce. Research shows that truants tend to become failures in their adult lives, experiencing more unemployment, more job changes and that they tend to lead unhappy personal lives.

Bullying

Governors need to consider from time to time what the school is doing to deal with bullying. Schools tend to underestimate the amount of bullying that takes place and primary schools tend to think it is a problem found only in secondary schools. Besag (1989: 49) found that the headteacher of one school where parents and children thought there was a serious problem, when asked about bullying, replied: 'There is no problem here, the parents and children are over-reacting'. A questionnaire to pupils asking whether they have been bullied gives a good idea of what is happening and the extent to which bullying is taking place. Bullying can go unnoticed because victims are often hesitant about telling staff that it is happening for fear of reprisals. Some bullying probably takes place in all schools and all schools need to take measures to outlaw it.

Ideally the school should have an anti-bullying policy. It should be discussed with pupils and they should be encouraged to protect younger and more vulnerable children. Teachers should be on the alert for pupils who seem reluctant to go out at break-times or those who seem to be loners or pupils who try to stay around adults. Pupils should be encouraged to report incidents of bullying involving themselves or others and these should be taken seriously, assuring the victim of support; such incidents should be logged on the files of both victim and bully. Parents of both victims and bullies should be involved. It is a good idea to bring victim and bully together and for the victim to say how he or she was made to feel and for the bully to say why he or she carried out the actions.

The needs of exceptional pupils

Governors need to check on what is happening for pupils with special educational needs and those who are exceptionally able who have their own special needs. All schools should have a special educational needs coordinator and it may be a good idea from time to time for the SENCO to come and talk to governors about the programme offered for children with special needs. The Code of Practice (DfEE 1994b) suggests that there should be a governor who liaises with the special needs department and keeps the rest of the governors informed about the work going on.

The coordinator for special needs may also have responsibility for exceptionally able pupils but it is probable that in many schools, no one has this responsibility. Governors need to ask questions about this area of work and encourage the school to make someone responsible and produce a policy and a register of pupils who come into this category.

A school can cater for the range of pupils by setting or streaming by ability. Generally speaking, streaming in which pupils are placed in a given form or class according to their ability for all their work is not very satisfactory because pupils vary in their ability in different subjects. A pupil may be good at mathematics but not very good at English. Many schools set pupils by subject so that a pupil could be in the top set for mathematics but the bottom set for English. The school needs to be aware of the effect of being in a low set on a pupil's self-esteem and the effect of low self-esteem on readiness to work. There is also the problem that teachers may underestimate how much pupils in a low set can actually do and may communicate unintentionally that not very much is expected of them.

An individual teacher can cater for the more able pupils by differentiating work in the classroom, giving work which makes differing demands to various ability groups within the class. This may involve the whole class learning about the same topic but individuals doing work matched to their ability or the pupils may be grouped with groups of different ability doing different work. Very able pupils may be given work which involves them in going more deeply into the topics being studied by the class. Another approach is to give open-ended topics to pupils which can be dealt with at a variety of levels. Clubs and societies may also provide opportunities for the very able pupils and it is valuable if they can be given opportunities to work with others of similar ability from time to time.

Equal opportunities

Governors need to ensure that there are equal opportunities for all pupils and that there is no unreasonable differentiation by gender, race, social class or ability.

The school should have an equal opportunities policy and this should be reviewed from time to time looking at how it is working in practice. Everyone has personal views about gender, race, social class and ability and these may include views which the person concerned would not like to express to friends and colleagues but which determine behaviour to some extent. Views about race, for example, are present in very young children and probably reflect the views of their parents.

Racism and multicultural education

Today's pupils are growing up in a society which includes many people of other races and cultures. A school may or may not have pupils of other races but all schools need to provide both multicultural education and antiracist teaching. Governors should question from time to time what is happening about this. It is too important a part of today's society to be left to individual teachers to do what they think best about it.

Gaine (1987: 10–11) makes the point that teachers tend not to believe that significant levels of hostility to other races exist, partly because they have not 'examined their own assumptions and preconceptions about race, immigration, and prejudice, so that the things that pupils say may simply not grate on their ears the way they would on another's'.

In a later book Gaine (1995) makes suggestions about the kind of in-service education which teachers may need, particularly in schools where there are few pupils from ethnic minorities. He suggests the following aims for multicultural/antiracist education:

- to raise awareness about multicultural education/racism in staff room discussion
- to prepare the ground for making our curriculum more multicultural (or effective in countering racism) where possible

- to try to clarify some concerns which have been troubling some members of staff
- to see if we are meeting the requirements of the National Curriculum
- to examine the relevance of multicultural perspectives (racism) in an all-white school.

(Gaine 1995: 106)

One important way of checking on whether pupils of ethnic minorities are doing as well as white pupils is to analyse examination and test results by 'race'. There will, of course, be some pupils in some schools who have a very limited knowledge of English and this will affect their performance but in many cases pupils who do not have English as their home language will have been developing their knowledge from the point when they started school and by the time they are at Key Stage 2 or 3 will be fluent.

Pupils will be learning about different religions in religious education and history and geography offer opportunities to learn about other societies. There should be opportunities to hear stories from other cultures and to study art and artefacts from other societies. But multicultural education by itself is not enough; there must be opportunities to consider and discuss attitudes to people of other races and cultures, so that pupils begin to see that people should be valued as individual persons whatever their background.

Gender

Boys and girls are different from birth. Girls acquire language earlier than boys and tend to enjoy language-related activities in school. They write more than boys and read more quickly. Boys tend to prefer mathematical, scientific and physical activity. Girls develop more quickly in childhood than boys but boys tend to overtake them in late adolescence. More boys than girls have special educational needs and at all stages in education girls tend to perform better than boys. In spite of this, research suggests that teachers tend to rate boys' ability slightly higher than that of girls.

Boys are often more demanding than girls and teachers need to be conscious of this and ensure that girls get their fair share of attention. Some mixed schools have experimented with single-sex classes for such subjects as modern languages where boys tend to do less well than girls.

Very few schools now give boys and girls different programmes but do both sexes have the same opportunities? Should the school be doing more to support the learning of boys? Examination and test results should also be analysed by gender.

Social class

Evidence from inspections suggests that some schools and teachers succeed in helping pupils from working-class backgrounds to achieve to a much higher level than other similar schools. This is partly a matter of expectation: one of the disadvantages of setting by ability is that teachers may have a low expectation of pupils, in the lowest sets and this may be evident to the pupils, who make less effort than they are capable of. Working-class parents may also have low expectations of what their children can achieve and the school needs to work with them to raise their sights and those of the pupils.

Pupils with special educational needs and disabilities

Teacher expectation is important where pupils with special needs and disabilities are concerned. Are children who would once have been in special schools achieving as well as they would have done in the special school environment? Once again low expectations may lead to less effort on the part of pupils. Governors also need to check whether less able pupils miss out on any of the opportunities the school offers. Are physically handicapped children, for example, able to join in as many of the activities which are offered as they are able? Do less able children have a chance to take part in drama productions?

Governors also need to be aware of the needs of the very able pupils, who may be held back by their slower classmates if attention is not given to provision for them.

Resources

Schools need to be aware of the impression which can be made by the materials and books which are used in school. What sort of impressions do the books that children are using give of different cultures, of male and female roles, different social classes and people with special needs? Are ethnic minorities shown in a positive light which counters stereotyped images? Are women shown in a range of roles and not just as wives and mothers?

Pupils' records

Governing bodies have certain duties with regard to pupils' records. The *School Governor's Manual* (Croner 1992–9) lists them as follows:

It is the duty of the governing body to:

(a) keep records on every pupil;
(b) allow access by parents and pupil (pupils over 16 and their parents are allowed access to their own records. Pupils over 18 are allowed sole access to their records);
(c) allow disclosure to other entitled persons;
(d) provide for correction or amendment if there are any inaccuracies, and ensure that a notice is appended if the holder of the record does not agree that the information is inaccurate, or misleading as to any matter of fact;
(e) delegate the day-to-day responsibility to the head and other teachers;
(f) consider all appeals against any decision by a head or teacher with delegated authority to refuse to disclose, transfer, copy or amend a pupil's record;

(g) arrange for a statement of the arrangements they made for the keeping and disclosing of records under their regulations to be available for inspection at the school;

(h) consider whether there is a need to translate the statement into a language other than English, and if so, have it translated;

(i) consider whether to make a charge for supplying a copy of the arrangements which should not exceed the cost of supply. The cost of a translated document should not be greater than the cost of the original document.

(Croner 1992–9: 6.88)

The school should not disclose anything in a record which involves another pupil, could harm the pupil concerned, relates to actual or suspected child abuse or gives information concerning a pupil's racial group, home language or religion.

Listening to pupils

Pupils are an important source of information about how the school is working and governors and teachers need to give thought to ways of tapping this. Schools for older children would be wise to have some form of school council or in the case of very large schools, a year-group council to which representative pupils can bring their concerns. Experience of a school council is also an important preparation for living in a democratic society. Junior children are well able to contribute to a school council and teachers need to give time to discussion with younger children about how they are experiencing school.

Some schools and classes, particularly in primary schools, are using what is known as 'circle time' to discuss problems that children are encountering in their everyday lives and to think together about ways of tackling them. Many of the problems will be to do with relationships and the discussion may involve considering alternative ways of acting. Circle time is also an opportunity for children to raise questions about aspects of school life which give them cause for concern.

Another way of finding out what pupils think about their school is to give them a questionnaire from time to time. Suggested questionnaires for Year 6 in the primary school and Year 7 in the secondary school are given in the Appendix.

Questions to consider

1   Are we happy with the present arrangements for admission of pupils? Is our standard admission number still valid for the school as it now is? Are we happy with the criteria we are using for decisions about admissions?

2   Is our behaviour policy resulting in pupils who are behaving well and becoming more self-disciplined? How many exclusions are being carried out during the year? Is the number decreasing?

3   How many unauthorised absences have there been in the past year? Are the numbers increasing or decreasing? What is being done to combat unauthorised absence?

4 How much bullying is there in the school? Have pupils been asked about it? What is being done when cases of bullying are brought to the attention of teachers? Do we have an anti-bullying policy?

5 Do we have a programme of personal, social and health education? What does it contain? What do pupils think about it?

6 Does our PSHE programme deal with health education and drugs?

7 Are we making adequate provision for pupils with special educational needs including the very able pupils?

8 Do we have an equal opportunities policy? Is it being implemented?

9 Do we have a policy on child protection? Who on the staff has responsibility for dealing with any cases which come to the school's attention? How many cases have occurred in the past year?

10 Do we listen to pupils' views about the school? Do we have a school council? What kinds of issues do pupils bring to it? Do they see it as an effective means of communication? Do any teachers use 'circle time'?

Chapter 11

Relationships with parents

The 1977 Taylor Report on the work of governing bodies makes the following comment about relationships with parents:

> The governing body should satisfy itself that adequate arrangements are made to inform parents, to involve them in their children's progress and welfare, to enlist their support, and to ensure their access to the school and teachers by reasonable arrangements.
>
> (DES and Welsh Office 1977: para 5: 28)

Schools need to be clear who is to be regarded as a parent. The Advisory Centre for Education's *Governors' Handbook* (1998: 7) states that:

> 'parent' in relation to a child or young person includes any person
>
> (a) who is not a parent but who has parental responsibility for him, or
> (b) who has care of him.

This suggests that the term 'parent' may include relatives or friends who have obtained a residence order from the court. Parents who have divorced keep responsibility even when the child does not live with them. Step-parents and unmarried fathers may also acquire parental responsibility.

Parents now have certain rights in law. Jones (1993: 44) lists these as follows: Parents, by law, can:

- express a preference of school for their children where this is practicable
- participate in the management of their children's school as elected parent governors
- attend an annual governors' meeting for parents and pass resolutions
- receive information about the school prescribed by statutory regulations, including the outcomes of assessment of existing pupils
- receive an annual report on progress made by their children, including plans of their work within the National Curriculum
- discuss this report with a named teacher at the school
- be consulted by governors on the provision of sex education at the school

- be involved, where appropriate, in the assessment and review of children with special needs
- in 1993, under new national arrangements for inspection, receive a summary of the inspection report and the governors' plans to tackle any problem areas
- have an opportunity to contribute their views to the inspection team.

Parents of children with special educational needs should be involved in the assessment and review of provision for their child.

Schools must make available to parents if required:

- inspection reports
- schemes of work currently used in the school
- syllabuses followed
- statutory instruments, including statutory orders for the National Curriculum
- a full copy of the arrangements for the consideration of complaints about the curriculum.

Parents also have a right to complain formally if they are dissatisfied with any aspect of the work of the school and the governors should ensure that their complaints procedures, both general and curriculum, are made known to parents. These will usually suggest a series of people to whom a parent can complain, starting with the class teacher in the primary school, the form tutor or the head of year or the head of department in the secondary school, going on to the headteacher and then the chair of governors and finally the LEA. Schools should record formal complaints (complaints in writing) and note what was done about them. It is wise also to record informal complaints which get as far as the headteacher. The *School Governors: A Guide to the Law* (DfEE 1997: 29) states that parents may use the curriculum complaints procedure if they believe that either the LEA or the governing body are failing:

- to provide the National Curriculum in the school or for a particular child
- to follow the law on charging for school activities
- to offer only approved qualifications or syllabuses
- to provide religious education and daily collective worship
- to provide the information they have to provide
- to carry out any other statutory duty relating to the curriculum.

As long ago as 1964 Douglas found that parents' interest in their children's schooling was an important factor in their progress and it is important that schools do all they can to ensure that parents work with them for the benefit of the children. Parents are their children's first teachers and should be regarded as partners in their children's education.

Atkin *et al.* (1988: 7) suggest that when parents

- understand what the school is trying to do
- identify with its main goals and support its efforts
- understand something of their role as educators

- take an active interest in, and provide support for their children's school work

then the effects can be dramatic and long-lasting.

Parents want to know about the school. They want to know about the curriculum, about examination and test results and the teaching methods being used in the school, about pastoral care of pupils, changes in education and the role of the governing body. They particularly want to know how best to help their child.

Parents are a considerable resource to a school. There is strong evidence that when parents of primary school children read with their children at home, the children make better progress in reading. Parental attitudes to school influence the children's attitudes. Parents may also have skills and knowledge which could be used by the school and there are many ways in which parents can help in school, which not only makes the teachers' tasks easier but also helps the parents concerned to understand what happens in school.

All governing bodies are in a strong position to hear parents' points of view in that there are parent governors on every governing body and their number has recently been increased. Parent governors are not delegates but representatives of parents and should try to keep in touch with the views of parents generally. Morrisey (1995) found that:

> Surveys at the school gate have indicated that, with a few exceptions, most parents have no knowledge of who the parent governors are, what they do on the governing body, and how they, as parents, can ensure that the places reserved for parent governors can best be used.
>
> (Morrisey 1995: 122)

Parent governors need to consider how best to let other parents know about the work of the governing body. It can help to have a governors' notice board at the school with photographs of the governors and copies of the minutes of meetings. The governors may have their own newsletter to parents or a section in the school newsletter. Some schools have experimented with the parent governors having a regular session at which parents can talk to parent governors and hear about the work of the governing body. This might be part of a PTA meeting.

The headteacher and staff of a school needs to have mechanisms for keeping in touch with parents. Many schools have a Parent–Teacher Association or its equivalent. Cyster et al. (1979: 32) found that the schools they studied saw the following as the aims of having a PTA or equivalent:

- to provide a close link between home and school
- to raise funds
- to give parents and teachers a better understanding of each others' problems
- to inform parents of the school's teaching methods and educational philosophy
- to provide a point of contact with the local community

A nursery school or a small infant or primary school has less need of a formal organisation than a large primary or secondary school, but all schools need mechanisms for keeping in touch with parents. Schools may do this through newsletters or there may be a case in primary schools for class meetings where the class teacher can tell parents what their children will be studying in the coming term or year and suggest ways in which they can help.

Home–school agreements

From September 1999 all schools have had to have a home–school agreement, a document in which the school, the parents (and in the case of older children), the pupil agree to support the pupil's education in various ways. The idea was put forward in the Standards and Framework Act of 1998, which defined the agreement as specifying:

- the school's aims and values
- the school's responsibility in relation to all pupils of compulsory school age
- parents' responsibilities while their children are registered at the school
- the school's expectation of its pupils.

The Advisory Centre for Education (1998) *Governors' Handbook* suggests that the home–school agreement should be seen in the context of a home–school policy and that there should be full discussion of it with parents. Parents should be given information on how to contact governors; parents of children with special educational needs should be told the name of the governor who liaises with the department for special needs.

Guidance on home–school agreements from the Department for Education and Employment (1998c) states that:

Agreements will work best when they are:

- a product of a genuine discussion between all the parties concerned, including the pupil
- balanced, fair and even-handed
- agreed, not imposed
- introduced as part of a whole school approach to working with parents
- clear and meaningful to parents: it is important to get the tone and style right so that all parties are clear about what is expected of them
- translated where the parent does not read English or communicated orally if the parent has difficulties with reading
- workable, not over-detailed and allowing for different family background and circumstances
- reviewed regularly.

(DfEE 1998c: 8)

Purposes of home–school agreements

The Berkshire paper *The School Compact* (Berkshire Education Department 1993: 3) suggests the following specific purposes for a home–school agreement. The paper suggests that the agreement can, for example:

> help parents to:

- know and understand what the school offers and what its goals are
- have easier access to the school and its staff
- believe they have a valued part to play
- take part in education in ways in which they are willing and able
- complement the work of the school by supporting their child's learning
- understand their responsibilities for pupils' attendance, conduct and work.

> help pupils to:

- gain as much benefit as possible from their schooling
- take increasing responsibility for their own futures
- respect and care for other people and their property
- understand their responsibilities for their work and behaviour, and for looking after their possessions
- sense that parents and teachers are consistent in the values they hold, that both are in broad agreement about education, and are prepared to work together in the interests of the child.

> help teachers to:

- improve their understanding of what parents feel about their child's education and so plan and teach more effectively
- provide the best possible education for pupils by enhancing what has been achieved at home
- maximise and make the best use of the resources available to the school
- fulfil their responsibilities for pupils' work, attitudes and behaviour.

Content of home–school agreements

The agreement has three parties (two for the younger children) the school, the parents and the child. The school section needs to cover:

- providing a broad and balanced curriculum
- providing a safe and secure environment
- helping each pupil achieve his or her potential and preparing him or her for the next stage of education or for adult life
- encouraging pupils to care for other people and for their surroundings
- providing suitable homework on a regular basis and marking it
- giving parents regular information about their child's achievement and progress
- keeping parents generally informed about school matters and being open to their views and concerns.

The parents' section needs to cover:

- taking an active and supportive interest in the school and in their child's work and progress
- supporting the school's behaviour policy and helping their child to achieve self-discipline
- ensuring that their child goes to school regularly and on time, properly equipped and (where appropriate) wearing the agreed uniform
- informing the school promptly in case of absence
- supporting their child in homework and other opportunities for home learning
- making the school aware of any problems likely to affect the child
- attending parents' evenings and discussions about their child's progress.

The pupils' section needs to cover:

- attending school regularly and punctually and being ready to learn
- endeavouring to do his or her best in all aspects of school life
- respecting the feelings and property of other people
- cooperating with teachers and abiding by the rules of the school
- wearing any school uniform and appearing tidy at all times
- behaving and acting in a way that reflects well on the pupil and on the school.

Some schools have printed the school's complaints procedure on the back of the home–school agreement. This is a useful way of making sure that all parents are aware of it.

Evaluating the effect of home–school agreements

The home–school agreement is not mandatory and some parents will choose not to sign such a document. This will give the school some indication of how the parents are regarding the agreement and of the general attitude of parents towards the school. There may be many reasons why a parent decides not to sign. Some may have difficulty in reading or writing English and may not understand the agreement. Some may just not bother and some may be intimidated by a formal document. The school needs to look at the proportion who do not sign and governors need to consider whether anything needs to be done to increase the numbers signing.

The agreement is a commitment on all sides to make certain provisions such as those listed above. Evaluating the effect of the agreement could involve looking at whether there has been any improvement in those areas. This would mean deciding what would be considered an improvement and looking for evidence.

The annual report and parents' meeting

The annual report

Since the 1986 Education Act governors of all schools are required to produce and send an annual report to all parents and hold a parents' meeting to present the report and discuss its contents. The report should be produced in other languages than English where this is needed. The 1986 Education Act laid down what should be included in the report. It should contain:

- the time, place and agenda of the annual parents' meeting
- a list of the governors and whether each is a parent, LEA, co-opted, foundation, teacher or staff governor
- the name and address of the chair of the governors and the clerk
- information about the next election of parent governors
- a statement of how the money available to the governors has been spent
- details of examination results (for secondary schools)
- a statement of links with the local community.

Schools need to find various ways to make the report interesting to parents. Some include photographs or reproductions of children's drawings or illustrate it in some way. It needs to be written in a style which is easy to read and if possible to include some personal accounts of the work of governors. One approach is to include brief reports from each of the main governors' committees, so that all the aspects of the governors' work is touched on.

Parents' meeting

Reports from schools across the UK suggest that the annual parents' meeting is not well attended and the House of Commons (1999) Select Committee paper on the role of school governors suggested that it should be dropped. This suggestion has not been accepted, however, and schools need to think of ways of making the event more attractive to parents so that more attend. Schools have tried such things as involving a speaker on a subject of general interest to parents, providing a short concert as part of the proceedings, showing a video or slides of the children at work or perhaps making it something of an open evening with children's work on show or an art exhibition. Governors might also present brief but interesting reports on aspects of their work such as the results of surveys involving children and parents, work done to improve the school premises or a description of how the governors set about the appointment of senior members of staff.

The meeting should give time for parents to ask questions and it is a good idea to ask for some questions in advance so that the headteacher or governors concerned can prepare to answer them fully. There should also be a chance to ask questions more informally as they arise from different parts of the meeting.

Reporting to parents on pupils' progress

Schools must give parents a report on their child's progress at least once a year by 31 July in Years 1–10 and by 30 September in Year 11 and provide an opportunity for them to discuss the report with a named teacher. Reports must give information about National Curriculum programmes of study, the levels the child has achieved and information about any examination results. Schools should also give comparative data about the achievements of children in the same year group, the same school and nationally.

There is considerable freedom given to schools about the form that the rest of the report takes but most reports contain information about attendance and punctuality, behaviour and involvement in extracurricular activities. Many reports give space for parental comment and this can form a basis for later discussion between teachers and parents; the school needs to retain a copy of the report.

The Qualifications and Curriculum Authority (1999a: 32) suggests that reports to parents should contain the following:

- Brief comments on the child's progress in each subject and activity studied as part of the school curriculum. These should highlight strengths and development needs.
- The child's general progress.
- Arrangements for parents to discuss the report with a teacher at the school.
- Total number of sessions (half-days) since the child's last report or since the child entered the school, whichever is later, and the percentage missed through unauthorised absence.

The QCA paper also suggests that parents should be told how their child's performance compares with his or her previous performance, the strengths and weaknesses, areas for development, how they can help and whether the child appears to be happy and settled and behaving well.

The actual format of the report also varies considerably from school to school. Some secondary schools use separate slips for reporting in each subject. This eases the problem of completing reports in that teachers are not kept waiting for someone else to complete their slot on the reports and it also avoids one teacher's report being influenced by what someone else has said. However, it creates problems for the form teacher, who has to assemble each set of reports. Some schools are using computers to help them complete reports with a choice of comment on the screen. This sounds rather impersonal but in secondary schools, the sheer pressure of time for completing reports, especially for teachers who teach a large number of pupils, makes some comments impersonal anyway and the use of computer generated comment may be helpful.

Goacher and Reid (1983) quote a headteacher commenting on the purpose of school reports:

> Its main functions, I suppose, should be encouragement and guidance of the pupil and to enable parents to form a balanced view of what happens to the child and how he is reacting academically, socially and culturally.
>
> (Goacher and Reid 1983: 23)

Goacher and Reid studied the views of a large number of pupils in secondary schools and found that 'Students were almost equally divided between the views that the report was useful in providing information about their progress in school, or that only some of the report was useful' (Goacher and Reid 1983: 78). They found a significant decrease in pupils finding the report useful as they grew older. Pupils wanted more advice on how to achieve better results and on the subjects they should take further; 80 per cent had discussed their reports with friends but over half had not discussed them with their teachers, while 92 per cent had discussed them with their parents albeit briefly. The majority claimed that after both good and bad reports they felt like working harder but some claimed that they would give up after a bad report.

Goacher and Reid (1983) also studied the views of parents; 85 per cent considered that the last report had provided a fair and accurate picture of the progress made by their child but over half of the parents felt that the report did not provide a complete picture of their child's progress.

> More than half felt that they were inadequately informed about their child's chances in public examinations, what the child was expected to learn in the various subjects, the nature of the teaching group in which learning was supposed to take place and, most marked of all, the child's future choice of career or prospect of further education.
>
> (Goacher and Reid 1983: 99)

This study is now somewhat dated, because the National Curriculum and regular testing have been introduced since then and schools now have to give test results and the achievement levels of the child's peer group. However, many of the points raised may still be relevant.

Governors need to be concerned with how the parents regard the school reports. Do they feel that the report gives an adequate picture of their child's progress? Is there any more information that they need? How do the pupils regard the reports?

Parents' evenings

Schools must run parents' evenings where parents can come and talk to teachers about their child's progress. Sometimes these involve the child as well but more often it is a meeting between parents and teachers. Bastiani (1989: 67) found that 'while both teachers and parents continue to support strongly the *idea* of the usefulness of such contacts, there is clear evidence that both find the actual *experience* of such events disappointing'. This is partly because time is limited but may be in some cases because the teacher is not prepared to listen to parents as well as telling them about their child at school. Teachers are usually not trained for this activity except through any training the school provides and young and inexperienced teachers in particular find the evening difficult.

Another problem that concerns parents is the lack of privacy for such meetings. They are very often held in halls or classrooms where it is possible for parents waiting to meet the teacher to hear the discussion with other parents. If it is at all possible the school should try to ensure greater privacy for such meetings.

Surveying parent opinion

Governors need to know what parents are thinking. There will be some feedback from parent governors and from the PTA but there is much to be said for canvassing a wider range of parents. A questionnaire might be sent to the parents of a whole year group of pupils or several year groups in a very small school. Different year groups can be canvassed at different times so that most parents sometimes get a chance to express their opinions. Suggested questionnaires are given in the Appendix.

Conclusion

Harding (1987: 52) lists some views of parents which highlight the barriers to good home–school communication:

* schools contact parents only when they want something
* insufficient time is allowed at parents' meetings for parents to discuss their child's progress with the teacher
* difficult to make private appointments to see the head or teacher
* PTA a small unrepresentative clique
* communication with parents of ethnic minority groups is frequently difficult and sometimes non-existent
* awareness of the school governing body is very low, and as a result the identities of parent representatives is frequently unknown.

Jones (1993: 49) suggests that:

A true partnership between home and school can bring about:

* positive attitudes
* positive self-image
* improved performance
* improved effort
* improved motivation
* support for teaching
* informed help from parents
* better parental understanding
* a shared purpose and belonging.

Questions to consider

1 Are we giving parents sufficient information about the school? Are we putting them in a position to support their child's education?
2 Do we have complaints' procedures in place and are parents aware of them?
3 Do all parents know who the parent governors are? What opportunities have parent governors to find out what other parents think?

4   Are we making as much use as possible of parents as a resource for the school?

5   Do we have sufficient liaison with the PTA?

6   Have we got a home–school agreement in place? What arrangements are we making to evaluate its effect?

7   How satisfied are we with our annual report? Could we make it more interesting to parents?

8   How many parents actually come to the annual parents' meeting? Could we make it more interesting so as to attract a larger audience?

9   How satisfied are we with our reporting system? Are parents satisfied with it? Could we improve it?

10 Do the arrangements for parents' evenings offer sufficient privacy for discussion with teachers? How well do staff manage these meetings? What do teachers and parents gain from them?

11 Would it be a good idea to survey parent opinion on different aspects of the work of the school?

Chapter 12

Marketing the school

Since schools are dependent for finance upon the numbers of parents who choose to send their children to them, it is essential that governors take seriously the building of a public image in the local community. Some governing bodies have a marketing committee which supports the efforts of the headteacher and staff in making the school known to parents in the locality but whether support is provided by a marketing committee or by some other group, governors must think about how the school sells itself. Even governors of a school which is the only one in the area cannot afford to neglect the school's external relationships.

A school relates to a number of different groups of people. Medgett (1996: 74) lists the 'clients' of a school as follows:

- current pupils and parents
- prospective pupils and parents
- staff and governors
- regular visitors and helpers
- the local community
- commerce and industry, both local and national
- local and national education authorities
- national groups and organisations.

Planning marketing

Governors need a plan for marketing the school which is well thought out and is revised annually.

Making an audit

A useful starting point where parents have a choice of school may be to discover what other schools in the area are doing. From this governors can go on to do a SWOT analysis – an examination of the strengths, weaknesses, opportunities and threats which face the school. A strength might be the current staff with perhaps a weakness in some particular area of curriculum, a building which does not serve the needs of twenty-first-century education very well or the school may be geographically in an unfavourable position to attract the full range of ability.

There may be opportunities to build on the contacts that individual governors provide, or to involve committed parents in supporting the school.

Next governors need to look at the arrangements already in place to market the school to parents and the local community. Foskett (1992: 14) suggests that schools need to consider the following questions about their external relationships:

1   Who are the internal and external audiences or stakeholders of the institution?
2   What external activities currently include or influence each of those stakeholders?
3   Who in the institution is undertaking those activities currently and what staff time and other resources are being applied to those processes?
4   What expenditure and income are involved in these processes?
5   How and by whom are the existing overall external relations being managed?
6   What resources, facilities, plant or staff-expertise – relevant to external relations are not being used to the full?

Governors may decide to survey parents to discover what might make them choose one school rather than others. A survey of new parents in one secondary school suggested that the wishes of the children themselves played an important part in which school was given as the parents' first choice and as a result of this the school went on to target Year 5 in the primary schools as well as Year 6 so that children thought about the secondary school at an early stage. The reason given by parents as the most important was 'We think our son/daughter will be happy there'. Other aspects which were seen as important were 'the enthusiasm of the teachers', 'the leadership of the school', and its facilities. Examination results were also seen as important but were not at the top of the list. A questionnaire similar to that used in this school is given in the Appendix. It supplied a good deal of useful information about what parents were looking for in a secondary school and enabled the school to target its publicity to meet the requirements of prospective parents.

Setting objectives

The next step is to establish some objectives. The school may want to increase the numbers of children applying for places or to attract a more representative range of pupils or to achieve additional funding for a variety of purposes. Governors may be concerned to help parents to become more informed about the work of the school so that they can do more to support their children's learning. Another objective might be to become more of a community school offering some services to the community as well as providing education for children. A secondary school may wish to enhance relationships with local industry so as to provide more places for work experience and to ensure that pupils from the school are seen by local employers as well educated and highly employable. Above all governors will want to enhance the reputation of the school.

It is important that the objectives set are widely agreed. All members of staff as well as the governors are ambassadors for the school as are the pupils;

objectives need to be shared so that both staff and pupils realise that they can make a difference to the way that the school is regarded in the locality.

Planning and implementing action

Once governors have established their objectives they need to go on to consider what funding they may require and who should take responsibility for the different aspects of the plan. Most of the funding will be in terms of time rather than directly in terms of money. If governors want to ensure that the local press represents their school well, someone has to produce press releases and follow them up with the local paper. If a secondary school wants to ensure that children and their parents in the local primary schools put it as their first choice, someone needs to spend time visiting local schools and talking to parents, teachers and children.

A useful starting point is to consider the image of the school which is held by parents and the local community. Foskett (1992: 159) suggests that: 'Every organisation has more than one image. It has the image it would like to project, it has the reality as it is perceived by those who work in it and it has the image that is perceived by those beyond its boundaries'. It may be useful to discuss the image of the school with staff, pupils and parents.

He goes on to suggest that there are four aspects of activity which reflect the school's identity:

1   The educational service provided.
2   The nature of the school environment.
3   The provision of information.
4   Behaviour and relationships.

(Foskett 1992: 162)

Everything that happens in the school has implications for its image and everyone needs to be aware of this. The school building and environment are part of the image. How does the school appear to someone coming to it for the first time? How does it appear from the outside? Is it difficult to find the way in? What sort of a reception does the visitor get? Is the inside of the school attractive in appearance? Does it convey something of the school's philosophy to a visitor? How helpful is the school when someone telephones?

The school's written communication also conveys an image. The first piece of written information which parents receive about a school is likely to be its prospectus. Does this reflect the values that the school stands for? Is it well produced and written in language that parents can understand? Does it include pictures of children at work? Is there an attractive letter heading with a logo used on all communication so that it is easily identified as coming from the school? Are letters and other communications written in a friendly, non-jargonistic style with translations where needed? Are they well laid out and good to look at?

The appearance and behaviour of pupils is a very important part of the school's image. Uniform tends to be attractive to parents and primary school pupils but not to older children, who do their best to stretch uniform rules to meet their idea of what is currently fashionable. However, it is part of the image of the school and pupils need to be told this and encouraged to look tidy. Their behaviour, particularly coming in and out of school, is very visible to the local community and affects the way neighbours of the school regard it. It is also important that pupils are encouraged to greet visitors to the school politely and helpfully. Pupils conducting prospective parents around a secondary school can make an impression which may determine the parents' choice of school for their child. Older pupils may also take a useful part in talks to parents who are trying to decide which secondary school to choose. Year 7 pupils may play a part in answering questions from Year 6 pupils in local primary schools.

The most important aspect of the school's image is the reputation it acquires as a school giving pupils a good education. Here relationships with the local media may be valuable. It is a good idea to send press releases to the local paper about school achievements and activities and if possible to get to know a reporter with whom the school can make contact when there is something to report. This person can be invited to school functions and encouraged to get to know the school. Contact with the media needs to be a responsibility for a particular member of staff who is a good communicator so that the reporter knows whom to contact if there seems to be a story. Local radio and television may also pick up information about an activity and feature it.

Schools naturally worry about pressure from the media when something bad happens but this should not stop a school from making contact when things are going well. Bad news is better seen against a background of positive achievement. If there is a disaster it is a good idea to act quickly to tell everyone an accurate version of what has happened and the action that is being taken to deal with the situation. There should be a decision at an early stage about who will deal with the media – usually the headteacher or the chair of governors.

Schools need to make links with local industry. In the primary schools children need to be helped to understand how things are made and done and the role of industry in the economy. There may be opportunities for schools to benefit from scrap materials from local industry. Primary schools can benefit from links with local services such as police, fire and ambulance which play an important part in community life. Secondary schools need links with local industry and services to provide opportunities for work experience.

Schools are part of the local environment which in turn offers opportunities for study at all levels. All schools need to involve pupils in studying their local history and geography and the economy of their neighbourhood.

Two important areas of external relationships are those between infant or first schools and junior or middle schools and that between primary and secondary schools. There is evidence that children tend to regress in their first year in secondary education and this must be partly because of the changes in approaches to learning in most secondary schools from that of most primary schools. The National Curriculum and the associated assessments should have made a difference to the problems of transition and schools must send on information about each child but the evidence suggests that there is still a good deal of repetition at the start of secondary education. This is partly because some secondary schools take from very large numbers of primary schools but also because teachers do not rate liaison with their opposite numbers very highly and many secondary school teachers like to start from scratch with their new Year 7s. In addition teachers in all phases tend to hold stereotyped and often outdated views about what goes on at the previous or next stage.

The link between infant or first schools and junior or middle schools and that between nursery and infant or first schools is often better, partly because the schools are often on the same site or geographically very near and also because junior and middle schools draw from fewer schools than secondaries. Governors should ask about the links between the phases of education and encourage teachers to make links with feeder or transition schools.

Gray (1992: 185) suggests that a marketing plan for the school should include:

- the establishment of marketing objectives and an organisational framework for marketing
- the systematic collection of marketing information through audit and research
- the development of a costed marketing plan that forms part of the school's corporate plan
- the implementation and evaluation of the strategies and tactics agreed in the plan.

Questions to consider

1 What arrangements do we have to communicate with each of our client groups?

2 What is our current expenditure in time and money on this communication? Is it sufficient? Can we afford to spend more?

3 What are our strengths, weaknesses, opportunities and threats?

4 Do we know the reasons why parents choose this school rather than others?

5 What are our objectives in marketing the school? Are these shared with all staff, parents and pupils?

6 What sort of an image does the school have in the neighbourhood? What image would we like it to have? What can we do to promote this?

7 Who is responsible for promoting the school's image in the area?

8 What part can pupils play in promoting the image of the school? Are they aware of the importance of the part they play?

9 What sort of relationship have we with the local press? Have we a contact with a local reporter who might promote our image? How often do we get publicity in the local paper?

10 What contacts do we have with local industry? What use do we make of these contacts?

11 What use do we make of the local environment for pupils' learning?

Chapter 13

Governor training

If governors are to achieve effectiveness, they need to be self-critical and make time to review the way they work, looking at the kinds of criteria listed in this book. Governors also need to take training seriously. One governing body made a survey of the training needs of its members using a pro-forma similar to the one shown opposite.

Most LEAs will make some provision for governor training and governors need to be encouraged to use such facilities as are available, particularly when they are new to the governing body. There is also much to be said for providing in-house training for the governors as a group. There may be skills among the members which can be shared with everyone; it may also be a good idea to get an outside speaker or leader for a day. A governing body may decide to spend a day or part of a day together looking at some problem which needs more lengthy consideration than there is time for at the normal governors' meetings. Time may be spent profitably reviewing the work of the governing body and evaluating its effect, perhaps using questions such as those given at the end of each chapter in this book. This kind of exercise has an additional value in helping to reinforce the feeling of being a team. It may also be a good idea to plan a joint working day with some of the staff.

Scanlon et al. (1999) carried out research into effective governing bodies and are quoted by Leslie (1999: 26) as saying: 'It was ... interesting that governors who were perceived as being effective often had some kind of training together as a group – perhaps a facilitator to come in and look at how they were operating. They worked well as a team'.

Scanlon et al. (1999) also found that heads of schools with highly effective governing bodies had a very positive attitude to their governors and an open management style which was participative and consultative. They believed that governors' commitment to the school was important – more important than special skills and expertise. Governors in this study emerged generally as committed, well educated and representative of their local communities, but schools that were socially disadvantaged and in inner-city areas had more difficulty in recruiting governors and reported lower levels of governor effectiveness.

An important part of governor training is the induction programme. The school needs to have in place good arrangements for helping newly appointed governors to become part of the team. Suggestions for the kind of information which a new

GOVERNOR TRAINING PROGRAMME

We should like to arrange an individual programme for each member of the governing body, which takes into account areas in which you are already knowledgeable and those in which you would like to learn further. We should therefore be grateful if you would complete the questionnaire below.

	Familiar with the area	Some knowledge but would like to learn further	Unfamiliar with this area
The National Curriculum and assessment			
Personnel issues – salaries, staff discipline etc. as they apply in schools			
Recruitment and selection of staff			
Special educational needs. Governors are responsible for the implementation of the Code of Practice			
School finance			
Religious education and collective worship. Legislation requires that all pupils take part and governors are responsible for the policy for this and for seeing that it takes place			
Post-16 education			
Target setting			

Are there any areas where you would welcome an opportunity to attend a training session or to discuss issues with someone more experienced?

Burgh Hill high school governors decided that they needed to offer an opportunity for members to practise the tasks involved in appointing new members of staff. They designed a job specification for someone in a senior post with special responsibility for staff development. They then invited three members of the staff who were applying for senior posts to act as guinea pigs. They would be given full feedback on their interview performance which should help them in future applications and would also have a chance to feed back to the interviewers their opinion of the interviewing. Each candidate had to write a proper application.

Nine governors decided they would like to take part and they divided into groups of three, with each panel given an area for interviewing. The areas chosen were staff development, the role of the form tutor and the teacher's curriculum role. Each group studied the application forms and planned the questions they would ask and decided who would ask each question.

The candidates were then interviewed by each panel in turn. At the end of the interviews each panel discussed the feedback they would give to the candidates, while the candidates discussed the feedback they would give to the interviewers. Representatives from each panel came together to form three new panels and each of the new panels gave feedback from all three interviews to one of the candidates. The candidates then met the interviewers together and gave their feedback.

governor will need were given in Chapter 1. It may also be a good idea to have a mentoring system for new governors, in which an experienced governor acts as an adviser to someone new to the role.

Questions to consider

1   How adequate are the skills and knowledge of our members for the task of governing the school?
2   Do we make enough use of the training opportunities available locally?
3   What provision do we make for the induction of new governors?
4   What training do we offer to newly appointed governors?
5   Do we know what training our members would like?
6   What in-house training opportunities do we provide?
7   Do we make time to discuss teaching and learning?

Chapter 14

Evaluation

Governors need to be concerned with how effectively the school is operating and how effectively the governing body is operating.

School effectiveness

There is a great deal of research into effectiveness in schools and effectiveness in individual teachers. Dean (1999: 5) has compiled lists covering the work of many writers on these two topics which may provide governors with criteria by which to judge the work of their schools. Research findings about effective schools include the following:

- There is strong leadership from the headteacher, who has a vision of what the school could be like, shares this widely and encourages others to contribute.
- All members of staff are committed to a shared vision for the whole school.
- The headteacher and senior members of staff lead in emphasising learning.
- Pupils' learning is at the core of all that the school does.
- The school climate is conditioned by high expectations about learning.
- There are clear goals which are commonly agreed.
- Decision making is a democratic process.
- There is trust among the staff and between the staff and headteacher, and teachers are not hesitant about consulting colleagues over problems.
- Achievement is characteristic of the whole school and is high year after year.
- There is order and discipline in the school.
- There is purposeful teaching and positive reinforcement for good work and behaviour.
- Pupils are given responsibility and self-esteem is fostered.
- Staff development is seen as important by all members of staff.
- There is systematic evaluation of all aspects of the work of the school.
- The environment has been made attractive and convenient for the work to be done.
- Parents are involved in the school and support its work.
- Governors have a clear idea of their role and that of the headteacher, and support the work of the school.

Research findings about effective teachers include the following:

- Effective teachers prepare well and have clear goals for their teaching.
- They aim to make as much teaching contact with all their pupils as possible.
- They aim to see that pupils spend as much time profitably on task as possible.
- They have high expectations for all pupils.
- They make clear presentations which match the level of the pupils.
- They structure work well and tell pupils the purpose of the work they are doing and the targets they hope the pupils will achieve.
- They are flexible in varying teaching behaviour and activities.
- They use many higher-order questions which demand thinking on the part of the pupils.
- They give frequent feedback to pupils about how they are doing.
- They make appropriate use of praise for both achievement and behaviour.
- They keep good records of the attainment and progress of individual pupils and these are shared and used. Progress in learning is constantly assessed.
- Their classrooms are well organised, ordered and attractive.
- They reflect on the work they and the pupils have done and evaluate progress towards goals.

Governors need to look for evidence of these characteristics. Classroom observation will demonstrate the extent to which teachers have clear goals, give good presentations, give feedback to pupils, ask questions which make pupils think and use praise effectively for work and behaviour. It will also be possible to judge whether classrooms are well organised. Discussion with teachers may also show whether they reflect on the work and evaluate progress towards goals. Some of these characteristics will also be evident if teachers regularly give talks to governors about their work, and test and examination results will give some information about the success the school is having in educating pupils. This information needs to be seen in the light of the general ability of the intake of the school and for many schools the important information will be the extent to which results are improving year on year.

Governors will be able to judge from the headteacher's regular reports and the school development plan the extent to which he or she has a vision for the school and this should in any case be shared with the governors who may also contribute to it. The commitment of members of staff to this vision will be evident in what they have to say to governors about their subject areas or classes.

Order and discipline will be evident in observation in the school and from the number of cases of exclusion which the headteacher brings to the governors. The school will also have a reputation in the neighbourhood as one which has good discipline or one which lets pupils get away with things. This may not be an accurate reflection of what actually happens but you need to be aware of it and also of the true state of things.

Governors should also be aware of the extent to which pupils are given responsibility in the school. Schools tend to give responsibility to those who show that they can take it, but those who need the experience to develop the ability to act responsibly tend to get less opportunity to acquire this skill. It can be useful to ask how pupils are selected for responsibility and whether there are some who are never given any responsibility. It is also useful to ask questions about how self-esteem is fostered, particularly in the less able and less well behaved pupils.

Ofsted (1997: 10) has studied schools which were failing and which have improved. Those which have improved most rapidly have

- strong leadership by the headteacher
- effective management by senior staff
- clear action plans with specific and measurable targets and outcomes
- committed teachers intent on improving matters
- good communication between the school and parents
- tackled poor behaviour and attendance satisfactorily
- developed plans for the National Curriculum and schemes of work for subjects
- effective financial management.

The effective governing body

The effective governing body:

- helps to create a vision which informs practice
- fosters a climate which supports effective teaching and learning
- ensures that members share responsibility and are able to contribute
- establishes a framework of principles and policies
- discusses, approves and monitors the budget
- has general responsibility for the premises and health and safety issues
- acts as a critical friend to the school and ensures accountability
- monitors the work of the school
- works in partnership with the headteacher and staff and supports their work
- represents the community and is in touch with the views of parents
- has an effective committee structure and effective meetings
- works as a team and uses the skills and knowledge of individual members
- plans training to meet the needs of its members.

Effective governing bodies hold effective meetings. Meetings are well prepared and well chaired and are of reasonable length. The aim should be a meeting of not more than two hours. Everyone should have received all the relevant papers in advance and should have read them, as well as having undertaken any action which was agreed at the previous meeting.

Governors also need to consider how far the subject matter of their meetings contributes to the achievement of the school. An Audit Commission (1990) study of school governors found that:

- Up to 50 per cent of the meeting time was spent in receiving information. This estimate did not include the information necessary for decision making.
- Between 45 and 65 per cent of the time was involved with operational matters.

- Only 10 to 25 per cent of the time was to do with performance review and policy making which the Audit Commission felt was potentially the unique and vital contribution which governors could make.

Holt and Hinds (1994) commenting on these findings suggest that:

> The governing body should make time to tackle the questions, 'How much do we think we are contributing to the effectiveness of the school?' and 'How well do we think we are doing as a team?'
>
> It will help the governing body to decide what things it needs to *advise* on, what *planning* and *policy making* is timely, what needs *coordinating* and which tensions need *mediating*, where the need is to *promote* and to *support*, and what particularly to *monitor*. It will reveal where the governing body needs to *improve its own working*.

(Holt and Hinds 1994: 33)

Questions to consider

1   How does our school measure up against the criteria for effectiveness given at the beginning of this chapter?
2   How do our teachers measure up against the criteria for teacher effectiveness?
3   How can we make judgements about school and teacher effectiveness? What evidence can we use?
4   How do we measure up against the criteria for governor effectiveness?
5   What difference do we make to the pupils' learning?
6   How effective are our meetings? To what extent do we discuss learning and curriculum issues?

Chapter 15

Conclusion

Every school should be aiming at improvement. Schools do not stand still. Some are improving, some are declining and some are just cruising, with everyone feeling satisfied with past performance. Governors should be concerned to see that their school is concerned to improve. No matter how good it is at present there are always areas for improvement and one measure of the effectiveness of a governing body is the contribution it makes to helping the school to improve.

Stoll and Fink (1996: 43) define school improvement as a series of concurrent and recurring processes in which a school:

- enhances pupil outcomes
- focuses on teaching and learning
- builds the capacity to take charge of change regardless of the source
- defines its own direction
- assesses the current culture and works to develop positive cultural norms
- has strategies to achieve its goals
- addresses the internal conditions that enhance change
- maintains the momentum during periods of turbulence
- monitors and evaluates its process, progress, achievements and development.

A school is more likely to improve if the ethos is good. Governors need to be aware of pupil and teacher morale and the extent to which teachers enjoy job satisfaction. The physical environment is important in providing a good context for teaching and learning. People work better when they are in comfortable surroundings and do not have to overcome problems posed by the building. Teacher–pupil relationships are an important reflection of the ethos of the school and this in turn is reflected in the quality of discipline. An essential for good school morale is good leadership where the headteacher and senior staff have vision and are seen by staff as being supportive and inspirational.

The Action for Governors' Information and Training (AGIT 1997) *Tool Kit* makes the following statements about the mutual expectations schools and their governors might have of each other:

> Governors and schools need to have a mutual understanding of and appre-
> ciation of one another. This need not be a mutual admiration but a recognition

of the problems each encounters, and of the contribution each brings to the partnership. Each need to recognise the boundaries and to be willing to re-negotiate these are circumstances change. Each must be accountable to the other in fulfilling its part of the partnership.

(AGIT 1997: 6.4/1)

School governors are now a very important element in the school. They have far more responsibilities than governors had in the past and the tasks are more demanding but the job is more rewarding in consequence. Governors can really make a difference. Good schools are those where head, staff and governors work in harmony and where governors are truly committed to seeing the school achieve and support the headteacher and staff so that this happens.

Appendix: questionnaires

YEAR 6 QUESTIONNAIRE

We should like to know how you feel about what has happened to you while you have been in this school and would be pleased if you would answer the following questions:

1 What have you really enjoyed while you have been in this school?

2 Has there been anything that you have really disliked?

3 Is there anything you have found particularly difficult?

4 Please tick ONE sentence which seems to apply to this school

Most of the teachers are friendly and helpful   ☐

Some of the teachers are friendly and helpful   ☐

A few of the teachers are friendly and helpful   ☐

5 Have you ever been bullied while you have been at this school? What happened?

6 If someone asked you about this school, what would you say?

7 We should like to know whether the views of girls and boys are different, so would you please tick the correct box.

girl ☐   boy ☐

YEAR 7 QUESTIONNAIRE

You have now been at this school for nearly a year. We should like to know how you feel about the school and would be pleased if you would answer the following questions:

1   What have you really enjoyed during the year?

2   Has there been anything that you have really disliked?

3   Is there anything you have found particularly difficult?

4   Please tick ONE sentence which seems to apply to you

A lot of our work this year repeated work we did in the primary school   ☐

Some of our work this year repeated work we did in the primary school   ☐

Most of our work this year was new to me   ☐

Please list any subjects which repeated primary school work

5   Please tick ONE sentence which seems to apply to you

I have worked really hard this year   ☐

I have worked fairly hard this year   ☐

I haven't worked very hard this year   ☐

6   Please tick ONE sentence which seems to apply to this school

Most of the teachers are friendly and helpful   ☐

Some of the teachers are friendly and helpful   ☐

A few of the teachers are friendly and helpful   ☐

7   Please tick ONE sentence which seems to apply to this school

   Most of the older students are friendly and helpful   ☐

   Some of the older students are friendly and helpful   ☐

   A few of the older students are friendly and helpful   ☐

8   Have you been bullied since you came to this school? If so, what happened?

9   Some people worry about homework when they transfer to secondary school. What do you feel about homework now?

10 If someone from your primary school who was choosing a secondary school asked you about this school, what would you say?

11 We should like to know whether the views of girls and boys are different, so would you please tick the correct box.

   girl   ☐   boy   ☐

YEAR 7 PARENTS' QUESTIONNAIRE

Your child has now been in the school for a year and we should like to know how well you feel that the school has met your expectations.

1   Please tick in the appropriate box to show how far you feel the school has come up to your expectations

    1   Our expectations have been substantially exceeded
    2   Our expectations have been exceeded
    3   Our expectations have been met
    4   We are a bit disappointed
    5   Our expectations have not been met

	1	2	3	4	5
The happiness of your son/daughter in the school	☐	☐	☐	☐	☐
The enthusiasm of the teachers	☐	☐	☐	☐	☐
The leadership of the school	☐	☐	☐	☐	☐
The care for individual children	☐	☐	☐	☐	☐
The good reputation of the school	☐	☐	☐	☐	☐
The behaviour of pupils in the school	☐	☐	☐	☐	☐
The liaison with parents	☐	☐	☐	☐	☐

Have you any other comments about any of these points?

2   In what other respects has the school come up to your expectations?

3   Are there any aspects of the school which have disappointed you?

4   Are there any aspects of the school about which you would like more information?

5   The governors and staff are keen to see the school go from strength to strength and maintain strong liaison with parents. Have you any suggestions for improvement?

Thank you for your help in completing this questionnaire.

PRIMARY SCHOOL PARENTS' QUESTIONNAIRE

Please tick the appropriate column

1   Our expectations have been substantially exceeded
2   Our expectations have been exceeded
3   Our expectations have been met
4   We are a bit disappointed
5   Our expectations have not been met

	1	2	3	4	5
Opportunities for parents to visit the school	☐	☐	☐	☐	☐
Reports you have received on your child's progress	☐	☐	☐	☐	☐
Opportunities to discuss your child's progress	☐	☐	☐	☐	☐
Opportunities to express your views and ask questions	☐	☐	☐	☐	☐
Information about the National Curriculum	☐	☐	☐	☐	☐
Information about teaching methods	☐	☐	☐	☐	☐
Provision for children with special educational needs	☐	☐	☐	☐	☐

Have you any other comments about any of these points? We should particularly like to know of any ways in which you have not been satisfied.

Thank you for your help in completing this questionnaire.

NEW PARENTS' QUESTIONNAIRE

Please tick the appropriate boxes to show your reasons for choosing this school

1   Important
5   Not important

	1	2	3	4	5
We have older children in the school	☐	☐	☐	☐	☐
The school is local and easy to reach	☐	☐	☐	☐	☐
Our son/daughter wished to attend this school	☐	☐	☐	☐	☐
The information provided by the school	☐	☐	☐	☐	☐
The facilities in the school	☐	☐	☐	☐	☐
The school was recommended by friends	☐	☐	☐	☐	☐
The examination results	☐	☐	☐	☐	☐
We think our son/daughter will be happy there	☐	☐	☐	☐	☐
We liked the 'feel' of the school at the open days	☐	☐	☐	☐	☐
The appearance of pupils in the school	☐	☐	☐	☐	☐
The behaviour of pupils in the school	☐	☐	☐	☐	☐
The leadership of the school	☐	☐	☐	☐	☐
There is ability grouping for most subjects	☐	☐	☐	☐	☐
The enthusiasm of the teachers	☐	☐	☐	☐	☐
There is a system for individual care of children	☐	☐	☐	☐	☐
The extracurricular activities provided	☐	☐	☐	☐	☐
The opportunities for physical education/sport	☐	☐	☐	☐	☐

Are there any other reasons for your choice of school?

Thank you for your help in completing this questionnaire.

Glossary

Admissions policy   Procedures used to decide entry to the school drawn up by governors/LEA

Agreed Syllabus   Each LEA through its SACRE draws up an Agreed Syllabus of religious education for its schools

ALIS   A Level Information System – predicts students' likely performance at A level based on earlier performance

Banding   System of organising secondary school pupils in broad ability groups

Catchment area   Designated area from which the school draws its pupils

Core subjects   National Curriculum subjects of English, mathematics and science

Criterion-referenced tests   Tests set against a predetermined standard rather than against statistical norms

Diagnostic testing   Testing to discover an individual pupil's strengths and weaknesses

Dyslexia   Serious difficulties in reading

Environmental studies   Studies concerned with the environment such as history and geography

Fair Funding   Scheme under which LEAs have to delegate the money available for aspects of administration to schools

Flash cards   Visual aids used to help young children with word and letter recognition

Form-entry   Number of classes in any one year group

Foundation subjects   National Curriculum subjects of art, design and technology, citizenship, geography, history, information and communication technology, modern foreign languages, music, physical education

Intelligence Quotient (IQ)   The score a pupil achieves on an intelligence test

List 99   List kept by the DfEE of teachers who must not be employed in a post involving children

Module   Unit of study within a course

Norm-referenced tests   Tests which measure pupils' performance against the performance of others rather than by predetermined criteria

Peripatetic teacher   One employed to work in several schools during the week

Sibling   Sister or brother

Standardised test   A test which has been tried out on large numbers of pupils to give norms for pupils of different ages

Supply teacher   Teacher employed on a day-to-day basis to fill absence of temporary vacancies

Vertical grouping   An organisation in primary schools where children of different ages are placed in the same class

Virement   Arrangement for moving spending from one category to another

YELLIS   Year 11 Information System – predicts pupils' GCSE results based on previous testing

Bibliography

Action for Governors' Information and Training (AGIT) (1997) *Tool Kit for Effective Governance*, Leamington Spa: AGIT.

Advisory Centre for Education (ACE) (1998) *Governors' Handbook*, 4th edition, London: ACE.

Askew, M., Brown, M., Rhodes, V., Johnson, D. and Wiliam, D. (1997) *Effective Teachers of Numeracy: Report of a Study Carried Out for the Teacher Training Agency 1995–6*, London: School of Education, King's Collage London.

Assessment Reform Group (1999) *Assessment for Learning: Beyond the Black Box*, Cambridge: Cambridge School of Education.

Atkin, J., Bastiani, J. and Goode, J. (1988) *Listening to Parents*, London: Croom Helm.

Audit Commission (1990) *We Can't Go On Meeting Like This*, London: Audit Commission.

Baginsky, M., Baker, L. and Cleave, S. (1991) *Towards Effective Partnership in School Governance*, Slough: National Foundation for Educational Research.

Bastiani, J. (1989) *Working with Parents: A Whole School Approach*, Windsor: NFER-Nelson.

Berkshire Education Department (1993) *The School Compact: Home and School Partnership*, Reading: Royal County of Berkshire Department of Education.

Berkshire Education Service (1997) *Effective Committees at Work*, Reading: Royal County of Berkshire Department of Education.

Berkshire Governor (1996) *Pupil Observers and the Governing Body*, Reading: Royal County of Berkshire Department of Education.

Besag, V.E. (1989) *Bullies and Victims in Schools*, Buckingham: Open University Press.

Black, P. and Wiliam, D. (1998) 'Assessment and classroom learning', *Assessment in Education*, 5(1): 7–74.

Charlton, C. and David, K. (eds) (1993) *Managing Misbehaviour in Schools*, London: Routledge.

Creese, M. (1995) *Effective Governors, Effective Schools*, London: David Fulton.

Croner (1992–9) *School Governor's Manual*, Kingston-upon-Thames: Croner.

Cyster, R., Clift, P.S. and Battle, S. (1979) *Parental Involvement in Primary Schools*, Slough: National Foundation for Educational Research.

David, K. (1993) 'Agencies working with schools', in C. Charlton, and K. David (eds) *Managing Misbehaviour in Schools*, London: Routledge.

Dean, J. (1999) *Improving the Primary School*, London: Routledge.

Deem, R., Brehony, K. and Heath, S. (1995) *Active Citizenship and the Governing of Schools*, Buckingham: Open University Press.

Department for Education and Employment (1994a) *The Education (Special Educational Needs) (Information) Regulations*, London: DfEE.

Department for Education and Employment (1994b) *Code of Practice on the Identification and Assessment of Special Educational Needs*, London: DfEE.

Department for Education and Employment (1995) *Circular 10/95: Protecting Children from Abuse : The Role of the Education Service*, London: DfEE.

Department for Education and Employment (1997) *School Governors: A Guide to the Law*, London: DfEE.

Department for Education and Employment (1998a) *The National Literary Strategy: Framework for Teaching*, London: DfEE.

Department for Education and Employment (1998b) *Education for Citizenship: Final Report of the Advisory Group on Citizenship* (Crick Report), London: DfEE.

Department for Education and Employment (1998c) *Home/School Agreements: Guidance for Schools*, London: DfEE.

Department for Education and Employment (1998d) 'Changes to the law on exclusion, education otherwise and discipline matters', letter sent by the DfEE on 8 May 1998 to headteachers, chairs of governors and chief education officers.

Department for Education and Employment (1999a) *(Circular 5/99:) The Induction Period for Newly Qualified Teachers*, London: DfEE.

Department for Education and Employment (1999b) *Circular 12/99: School Teachers' Pay and Conditions of Service*, London: DfEE.

Department for Education and Employment (1999c) *The National Numeracy Strategy: Framework for Teaching Mathematics from Reception to Year 6*, London: DfEE.

Department for Education and Employment and Qualifications and Curriculum Authority (1999a) *The National Curriculum in England: English*, London: DfEE and QCA.

Department for Education and Employment and Qualifications and Curriculum Authority (1999b) *The National Curriculum in England: Mathematics*, London: DfEE and QCA.

Department for Education and Employment and Qualifications and Curriculum Authority (1999c) *The National Curriculum in England: Science*, London: DfEE and QCA.

Department for Education and Employment and Qualifications and Curriculum Authority (1999d) *The National Curriculum in England: Citizenship*, London: DfEE and QCA.

Department for Education and Employment and Qualifications and Curriculum Authority (1999e) *The National Curriculum in England: Music*, London: DfEE and QCA.

Department for Education and Employment and Qualifications and Curriculum Authority (1999f) *The National Curriculum in England: Physical Education*, London: DfEE and QCA.

Department of Education and Science (1991) *Education (Pupils' Attendance Records) Regulations*, Statutory Instrument 1991/1582, London: DES.

Department of Education and Science and Welsh Office (1977) *A New Partnership for Our Schools* (Taylor Report), London: HMSO.

Douglas, J.W.B. (1964) *The Home and the School*, London: Macgibbon and Kee.

Earley, P. (1994) *School Governing Bodies: Making Progress*, Slough: National Foundation for Educational Research.

Esp, D. and Saran, R. (1995) *Effective Governors for Effective Schools*, London: Pitman.

Foskett, N. (ed.) (1992) *Managing External Relations in Schools*, London: Routledge.

Gaine, C. (1987) *No Problem Here: A Practical Approach to Education and 'Race' in White Schools*, London: Hutchinson.

Gaine, C. (1995) *Still No Problem Here*, Stoke-on-Trent: Trentham.

Goacher, B. and Reid, M. (1983) *School Reports to Parents*, Windsor: NFER-Nelson.

Gray, L. (1992) 'Marketing the school as an educational institution', in N. Foskett (ed.) *Managing External Relations in Schools*, London: Routledge.

Harding, P. (1987) *A Guide to Governing Schools*, London: Harper and Row.

Holt, A. and Hinds, T. (1994) *The New School Governor: Realising the Authority in the Head and Governing Body*, London: Kogan Page.

House of Commons (1999) *The Role of School Governors*, Paper no. 5091, London: HMSO.

Jones, J. (1993) *What Governors Need to Know 3*, London: David Fulton.

Keys, W. and Fernandez, C. (1990) *A Survey of Governing Bodies*, Slough: National Foundation for Educational Research.

Knight, B. (1993) *Financial Management for Schools: The Thinking Managers Guide*, London: Heinemann.

Leslie, H. (1999) 'Wise head rests on a strong body', *Times Educational Supplement*, 25 June.

Maychell, K. (1994) *Counting the Cost: The Impact of LMS on Schools' Patterns of Spending*, Slough: National Foundation for Educational Research.

Medgett, D. (1996) *Publicising Your School*, Oxford: Heinemann.

Medwell, J. Wray, D., Poulson, L. and Fox, R. (1998) *Effective Teachers of Literacy: Report of a Research Project Commissioned by the Teacher Training Agency*, Exeter: University of Exeter.

Morrissey, M. (1995) 'A parent response', in D. Esp and R. Saran, *Effective Governors for Effective Schools*, London: Pitman.

Mortimore, P., Sammons, P., Stoll, L., Lewis, D. and Ecob, R. (1988) *School Matters: The Junior Years*, London: Open Books.

National Advisory Committee on Creative and Cultural Education (1999) *All Our Futures: Creativity, Culture and Education*, London: Department for Education and Employment.

Ofsted (1997) *From Failure to Success: How Special Measures are Helping Schools Improve*, London: Ofsted.

Ofsted (1999) *Standards in the Secondary Curriculum*, London: Central Office of Information.

Potter, E. and Smellie, D. (1997) *Employment of Staff: A Guide for Governors*, Kingston-upon-Thames: Croner.

Qualifications and Curriculum Authority (1999a) *Assessment and Reporting Arrangements at Key Stage 2*, London: QCA.

Qualifications and Curriculum Authority (1999b) *Qualifications 16–19: A Guide to the Changes Resulting from the Qualifying for Success Consultation*, London: QCA.

Scanlon, M., Earley, P. and Evans, J. (1999) *Improving the Effectiveness of School Governing Bodies*, London: Department for Education and Employment.

Strudwick, H. (1999) 'Ignorance is not an option', *Times Educational Supplement*, 3 December.

Weston, P. (1999) *Homework: Learning from Practice*, London: Ofsted, HMSO.

Index

National Literacy Strategy (NLS) 71
National Numeracy Strategy (NNS) 73
National Professional Qualification for
   Headteachers (NPQH) 96
newly qualified teachers (NQTs) 96
newsletters 41
number 72;
   across the curriculum 74
numeracy;
   hour 73;
   effective teachers of 74

objectives 19, marketing 122–3
observation of teaching 42–5
Office for Standards in Education (Ofsted)
   38–40, 55, 69, 75, 77, 80, 86, 131, 133
Ombudsman 101

parent-teacher association (PTA) 48, 50,
   112
parents 101, 102, 104;
   annual report to 10, 23, 29, 31, 35, 39,
   41, 55, 86;
   annual meeting 23, 31, 35, 55, 116;
   definition of 110;
   evenings 36, 48, 118;
   of pupils with special educational needs
   57;
   relationships with 31, 110–120;
   rights 110–11;
   surveys 119, 122
parent governors 3–6, 9, 112
parent partnership 119
pastoral care 79
pay, teachers' 59, 89–90
pensions, teachers' 98–9
performance management 90–1
person description 91
personal, social and health education
   (PSHE) 14, 3, 54, 79, 81, 109
personnel/staffing 7, 24, 30–1
physical education (PE) 13, 14, 78
play 68
policy 39;
   able pupils 59;
   admissions and appeals 20;
   anti-bullying 59, 104;
   assemblies 59;
   assessment and recording 58, 86;
   behaviour 22, 24, 54, 56, 102;

careers education 59;
charging for school activities 20, 55;
child protection 20;
complaints 50, 57, 96, 111;
curriculum 14, 20, 52, 54, 55–6;
employment 20;
English 71;
equal opportunities 22, 52, 54, 58,
82;
framework for 52–5;
health and safety 53, 56;
health education 20, 59;
homework 59;
implementation of 53–4;
legally required 20–21, 52, 55–8;
lettings 32, 59;
literacy 70, 87;
making 52–9;
marking 58;
numeracy 87;
pay 59, 89–91;
pupil discipline 10, 20, 102;
pupil records and reports 20, 86;
religious education 20;
reviewing 34;
sex education 21, 58;
special educational needs 16, 21, 53, 54,
57;
staff discipline and grievance 55,
56;
staff development 59;
staffing 57;
uniform 59
post-16 education 8
Postgraduate Certificate of Education
   (PGCE) 89
Potter E. and Smellie, D. 98
premises 21, 24, 38;
   committee 30, 32
problem solving 83
professional organisations 98
prospectus 123;
   contents 19–20, 37, 86
public relations 23, 24, 121–5
pupils 114;
   appearance 49, 123–4;
   behaviour 37, 44, 49, 123–4;
   behaviour policy 22, 24, 54, 56, 102;
   with exceptional ability 58, 104–5;